WWFD?

What Would Fred Do?

A conversation about friendship and being an advocate for children.

¿Qué haría Fred?

Una conversación sobre la amistad y ser un defensor de los niños.

by/por Todd Cole,

Teacher of Masterpieces

Maestro de Obras Maestras

First printing 2026
Printed in the United States of America
Primera impresión 2026
Impreso en los Estados Unidos de América

Tree Shadow Press

Tree Shadow Press
www.treeshadowpress.com

ISBN: 978-1-948894-47-0

Dedication

For Ellen
Para Ellen

Thank you for being an instrument of the good who sparked and fostered my friendship with Fred.

Gracias por ser un instrumento del bien que encendió y fomentó mi amistad con Fred.

Foreword

What would Fred Do? As a friend of Fred Rogers, I am writing possible answers to this question from my history with this kind, gentle, thought-provoking, minister for children (and adults). I write this book, not to capitalize on my relationship with Fred. I am writing this book more for me than for you.

In troubling times, I believe we all look for answers to questions of how we can move forward. I had a need to write these thoughts in order to help me become a beacon of Fred's light. If it helps you to do the same, that is "icing on the cake."

What a gift it will be for me if my explanation of different seasons of my friendship with Fred Rogers (mostly through letter writing) helps YOU to expand your mission to become a better human…a committed adult for children who are our leaders of tomorrow.

To provide you with some background, I am a retired elementary school teacher with 25 years as a teacher of first graders and 9 years as a teacher of fourth graders. Upon retirement, I switched gears and began teaching college students who had a calling to become teachers. I have had this opportunity at my Alma Mater, Westminster College, in New Wilmington, Pennsylvania.

I walk down the same hall that I once walked as an undergrad from 1979 to 1983, but this time, I sit on the "other side of the desk." This is both a privilege and honor to bring "first-hand experience" to those who will enter the most noble profession in the world…teaching children.

May my simple, yet sincere, words guide you, as they have me, to question HOW I, and hopefully you, can become a better neighbor.

TABLE OF CONTENTS

CHAPTER ONE

Our Friendship from the Beginning

It's critical to "set the stage" of how Fred became a huge influence on my life as an educator and human being. Knowing how our friendship evolved will help you to understand how I have come to answer the question, "What would Fred do?" So, here it goes.

It all began with a project my first graders sent to "Mister Rogers" in the 1980s. Because my school district was a part of the Western Pennsylvania map, my students had prior knowledge of Mister Rogers' Neighborhood on WQED in Pittsburgh. It was our first "book publication" for the school year, "Our Rule Book" written by The Masterpieces of Museum 106."

I referred to my students as masterpieces and the classroom as a museum. Each student wrote a "rule" and drew an illustration to explain the rule. Then, each rule was copied and made into a book using my Binder Machine that joined each rule together with a plastic coil binder on the left side of the book. Each child received their own copy. We read the book aloud several times, before sending it home to add to their Home Library of books to read with their family. We sent a copy of the book to Mister Rogers, and then the rest, as they say, is history. (By the way, my first graders would write more than 20 books a year and I'd often find the books on display at their high school graduation parties. You never know how important the written word of a child can be in their fabric of life.)

Mister Rogers, (note that I wasn't calling him "Fred," yet), quickly responded with a letter on Mister Rogers' Neighborhood stationery. He wrote of how rules are important in life in order to keep us safe. He shared his appreciation for how each student held their pencil so carefully in order to draw pictures to represent each rule. Can you imagine the thrill each child felt knowing that Mister Rogers appreciated how they held their pencil?

It's so important for me to acknowledge how Mister Rogers drew attention to something so simple and yet so important to a first grader and their teacher. You need to know that this is what makes teachers/theorists/ministers and Mister Rogers SPECIAL to young children. People in the "field of helping young minds grow" will THINK about what is important to their audience and then acknowledge it in an age-appropriate way. Mister Rogers was an expert in addressing what's essential to the EVERY DAY life of a young child…holding a pencil, correctly, was one of them.

Needless to say, I made a copy of the letter for every child and we framed the original and placed it on top of our classroom library bookcase.

From there, Mister Rogers and I became personal pen pals, and at some point (with the assistance of my friend, Ellen), he called to invite me to his "neighborhood" for a taping of his half-hour program. I took a "personal day" and drove to WQED in Pittsburgh, Pennsylvania. This was about an hour and a half away from my home.

I remember my attire. It was a blue blazer and khaki pants with a SAVE THE CHILDREN tie. (I still have them.) I was a nervous wreck. I had never driven to Pittsburgh. I left my home extremely early in fear of getting lost and being late…I remind you that this was before cell phones and Map Quest.

I arrived an hour early, so I had ample time to either calm my nerves or accelerate them (you pick). When I gained the courage to enter the building, I was given instructions to ask for Hedda. She quickly came to my rescue to greet me with a smile that shined and eyes that said "welcome" before she even said a word. She extended her hand which was met with the sweaty palm of mine, but she didn't seem to care. As we walked to THE LAND OF MAKE BELIEVE, she shared with me that Fred was eager to meet me "face to face."

Oh my. One of my heroes was eager to meet ME?

Of course, I was beyond excited to meet an Icon for Children, but the fact that he was eager to meet me, made me feel "special." This, as we all know, was one of Mister Rogers' messages…everyone is special just the way they are.

As she escorted me into the studio, there it was. The castle was resting at eye-level to my left of the studio with the tree in the center and the clock to its right. Off to the right was a grand piano and along the wall were spools that displayed the puppets Mister Rogers used during various segments of the show. The Land of Make Believe was bright and beautiful. I hope I have "painted the picture" accurately. As I get older, I have come to realize that some parts of my memory are "challenged."

They were in the middle of rehearsing a segment with X the Owl. I stood several feet from the tree. There were several chairs set up that seemed to be for guests, so I assumed that one of the chairs would be for me. Mister Rogers was kneeling behind the tree with the "X the Owl" puppet.

Suddenly, Mister Rogers looked over at me. He stood up and moved from behind the tree. Fred, dressed in all black, clothing color for puppetry, was suddenly in front of me. He extended his hand that soon turned into a cupholder for both of my hands.

Then, he pulled back making direct eye-contact and said, "Oh my. What a pleasure it is to meet you." Then he announced, "Everyone, this is Teacher Todd, Teacher of Masterpieces and my friend."

I truly can't remember what happened next, but I eventually found myself hiding behind the tree with Mister Rogers, holding his script as he read the part of X the Owl. My hand was shaking as I held the stapled pages of dialogue, but Mister Rogers never called attention to my nerves. I was, literally, shoulder to shoulder with him, on our knees, for the tree width wasn't all that wide. We had to be hidden from the camera's view.

To be honest, I was a bit uncomfortable being this close to another human that I didn't know too well…but actually, I guess I did know him. He was "everyone's neighbor." Later on, I would learn that there would be one more "uncomfortable moment" that I would eventually "long for and expect" when we met from time to time, but I don't want to "get ahead of myself."

When this portion of the taping concluded, Mister Rogers walked me to his piano as he played a bit of whimsical improvisation that signaled to his team that taping had concluded until the afternoon. I was in awe of his piano skills. It came so naturally to him. I, too, used the piano in my first-grade classroom as a form of "transition" from one event to another. I was fortunate to have the extra piano from the music department in our elementary school in my classroom. I often played a tune on the piano and told my students that once the piano-playing stopped, they were to have their reading books, on their desks, opened to the first page of a given story.

Back to my visit at WQED…I was looking around at everything that was a part of the "magic" in the Land of Make-Believe, when Mister Rogers concluded his masterpiece and smiled at me saying, "Music is such an important part of my life." He knew I had a love for music, for I had written to him about singing in the church choir. After he played his masterpiece on the piano, I managed to share how I played the piano in my classroom. He asked me to explain it further, so I tried.

When I say "managed" and "tried" you need to understand that I was speaking with a hero whom I cherished, and it was a bit overwhelming. His genuine thirst to know more about me seemed to make further discussions to be more relaxing.

He walked me to his puppets as he placed X the Owl on its assigned home (spool). He shared a few of them with me. He became the character as he placed each puppet into his hand. It was so enchanting. My eyes were wide and my heart was full as I realized I was in the presence of a Leader for Children (and their parents). His love for puppetry was obvious as he looked at each puppet that he placed on his hand. Each puppet brought a different tone of voice, and yet the smile on Mister Rogers' face as he became each character was the same ...his eyes and facial expressions lit up the room. He was in his "element." I saw complete joy on his face. It was also clear to me that he took pride in what he had created as he shared a few of the puppets with me.

What a special moment!

I neglected to mention that other puppets, held by other puppeteers, were introduced to me when I had the honor of sitting on the floor (cross-legged) behind the castle during another part of the taping. One of the kind men, in particular, was Lenny. He "played" Prince Tuesday. I never met him again, but he made a positive impression on me for being a kind, gentle soul. Mister Rogers spoke of him, kindly, in a few of our future correspondences. Mister Rogers spoke of

Lenny's involvement with musicals, for Fred knew of my work with my district's high school musicals as the choral director. I hope Lenny reads this so he realizes the impact that our brief encounter had on me. I'd love to meet Hedda again, too. She was such a kind greeter.

Anyway, after the awe-struck moment with the puppets, Mister Rogers walked me to his office. It was a very unpretentious office…one might call it cluttered. I tend to share the "cluttered gene" as a teacher. I've been told that it's a sign of creativity…so let's go with that. I assume that most of Mister Rogers stacks contained fan mail to be personally acknowledged by the Master of Letter Writing, Mister Rogers, and scripts and music for future segments. He often wrote to me about his "next project."

While in his office, we talked. It wasn't "small talk." He wanted to know everything from my philosophy of education to my personal life. Much of my life had already been shared through letters. It was a long conversation that I eventually learned would last a lifetime. But it was at that moment "Mister Rogers" became "Fred" to me. Meetings and many phone calls and letters would follow. I would share my relationships about my parents and my best friend with him. I'd find myself sharing concerns about my students to which he would provide comforting words and encouragement.

I continued to have my students write to him on a yearly basis, and he would respond with his authentic written words that would provide a meaningful memory for each of my students for many years to come. But it would be my personal friendship with Fred that would help me put "life's events" into perspective and assist me in each "season" of my life's journey.

*After our first meeting on set of The Land of Make Believe and grace-filled visit in his office, I received a letter from Fred.

Here is a portion of his words:

"Dear Todd,

After we finished taping yesterday, I came up to the office and found the above in the chair where you had sat during our visit."

Fred had taped a dime to the top of the letter. He had found a dime sitting on the cushion of the seat. Isn't that the epitome of what Fred was all about? He couldn't let something as small as a dime be left without returning it to its owner.

That's "what Fred would do."

Chapter Two
Being Alone

I once shared my yearning to be married and have children in a letter to Fred. I felt that having a family was the "normal," "expected" thing to do. As a single man, it's odd to be at functions that center around "family." I went through a time when it made me feel uncomfortable and isolated. Fred once wrote to me, "You mention a wife and child and wishing for that. I just want you to know that we know quite a few "single" people who live most fulfilling; other-oriented lives. In fact, my major professor, Dr. Margaret McFarland was one such person. Her dedication to her students and her child development studies (as well as her nieces and their children) took up all of her waking hours. She made an enormous difference in many people's lives."

He went on to share stories about teachers in his life as an elementary student who never married and "decided early on that they wouldn't have husbands and children, but would dedicate themselves to their educational work."

He ended that portion of the letter by saying, "Somehow I felt the need to reflect that to you." So, to answer the question, "What would Fred do?" He allowed me the grace I needed to understand that "alone" is different than "lonely." I think being alone has turned out to be one of my most endearing qualities. It's a luxury that most people can't afford. (Remind me of this the next time I feel lonely.)

All kidding aside, Fred's words gave me the courage to be more comfortable in my own skin. I knew I wanted to be the best teacher I could be. Fred helped me to understand that every person has his or her own unique journey. My choice to follow a road less traveled, without my own children, was what made/makes me who I am. I knew I couldn't separate my life's work from a personal life that would need to be "shared." That being said, I marvel at all of my colleagues who have been able to balance their passion for teaching with a love for raising a family. I am amazed and grateful for their example. I just knew it would be too difficult for me. Many colleagues and friends would tell me that my students were "my kids."

I'd like to think so, too.

For an example, I just returned from having dinner at a local restaurant where I, unexpectedly, sat next to a husband and wife…the husband was one of my first graders from years gone by. I hadn't spoken to him in years, but he recognized my voice as I spoke with my waitress, so he started up a kind conversation. During our discussion, I learned it was his birthday and his wife had just accepted a job as a special education teacher. What a delight it was to catch up on the life of a past student! It made my evening. I quietly asked my waitress to put their dinners on my tab. My gesture was a small token for brightening my life and honoring me with the opportunity to teach him when he was in first grade.

You will soon find out that my students, colleagues, my own parents/brother, neighbors and lifelong college friends would become the blessing of what I call "family." Fred was/is a part of that family.

So being alone has turned out to be a fabric of comfort for me. Of course, Titan, my golden retriever, is lying next to me as I type these thoughts…so I'm not completely alone. Plus, I have my music. I appreciate listening to my favorite singer, Sandi Patty, as I work and drive in my car.

Maybe being alone will change, someday, but for now this is my happy place.

Chapter Three

Loss

During a conversation with Fred in his office, I recall a man coming in to speak with Fred. I recognized the voice as being very familiar, but his back was in front of me and he was in "street clothes." Fred had to introduce us. It was David Newell, aka Mr. McFeeley. I stood up from my chair and shook his hand. Embarrassingly, I didn't let go. I kept on shaking his hand. Eventually, I let go with no request from him. We all laughed that I didn't recognize him without his Speedy Delivery Attire. David and I "reconnected" many years later. You'll read about that in an upcoming chapter.

After David left, I soon realized that Fred was becoming part friend and part counselor. Why? Well, at one point there was silence in the room. Silence is always a key strategy for counselors to use. It was as if Fred was waiting for me to guide the discussion. It was at this point that I shared with him my concern for one of my students who lived in a small trailer with her mom.

Katlyn, my student, was bright and beautiful. She didn't know of her father for he was not "in the picture". This happened frequently in my classroom. I would receive my roster at the beginning of the year with several student names that listed a mother without a father. These students were often placed in my room by request of their mothers. It was an honor to be a "father figure" for these students. As a first-grade, male teacher, I always felt a responsibility to be a role-model for children who didn't have a father living in their homes. Many of you know, teachers wear many hats…and "parent" is one of them.

This was an extra special student. Katlyn lived across the street from her grandmother who was very involved in her life. One morning, my little first grader's mommy didn't wake up. She had died in her sleep. I shared this tragic event with Fred. We talked about the need to be "present in her life."

Teaching the Alphabet Sounds and Number Recognition seemed so insignificant at times like this. Fred and I spoke of the connection we make as educators with our students that make learning possible. Fred, during his television segments, had a way of making a personal connection with his listeners. He was so skilled in reaching each child on a personal level as he looked into the camera. Sometimes this connection allows for lessons that are "outside the curriculum's textbook."

It's important to note that primary teachers spend more waking hours with students than the parents of their students during the school day. Bedtime for primary age kids is (hopefully) around the 8pm to 9pm hour, thus leaving the longest period of waking hours to be at school with their teachers. Teachers, truly become a "second parent" to many. I, as many teachers will attest, have been called "Mom," "Dad," "Grandma," or "Grandpa."

That's a compliment.

Katlyn's transition without her mommy was a difficult season in her life. I'd like to think I helped her through some of the questions and fears she had at the beginning of her journey with grief. Fred wrote to me after our discussion about loss.

He wrote, "How blessed they (Katlyn and her family) are to have you in their life right now!"

It's just another reminder that so much of what a teacher has in his toolbox is from a personal connection developed between teacher and student…I refer to it as The Textbook of Life.

It was in the same letter that Fred shared the death of his musical director, Johnny Costa. "As you can imagine we miss him greatly. Next Thursday begins studio taping. It'll be the first time in 30 years I'll have to walk into the studio without his "physically" being there." I sent Fred flowers and he, in true Fred Fashion, took a Polaroid photo of them and sent the photo to me in a letter of thanks. Polaroid Cameras were a "thing of the past," but not to Fred. (Although, they do seem to be making a comeback.) It was not the only time I received a Polaroid photo from him. The Polaroid camera was his "go to."

As I reflect, Fred was a busy man. He didn't have extra time to travel to the Foto Mat (the small drive-up film development "hut" that could be found in the center of shopping strip mall parking lot). Am I aging myself? Anyway, Polaroid Cameras allowed Fred to have instant photos that he could send to people like me.

Another loss our school experienced was of a dear student of mine who died of meningitis. His name was Robby. It was sudden. It wasn't like a cancer diagnosis where you had "time" to accept the predicted course of treatment. It was so difficult to process. I found out of his death through our "phone chain" that was used by the faculty when we would have a Snow Day. I was in disbelief. I found myself asking my colleague on the phone to repeat the news of the tragedy. It just didn't seem possible.

I had Robby in first grade, but he died when he was in fifth grade. Robby had such a zest for life. I was heartbroken, as were all who knew him. I had a special friend, Ellen (see Dedication Page) who contacted Fred to let him know what had happened.

Fred called as soon as he found out. Words of comfort came pouring out over the phone. Although I had not seen Robby on a daily basis since he left first grade, he continued to drop off a Christmas Ornament for me when he was in second, third, fourth, and fifth grade. His mother continued the tradition, after his death, until what would have been Robby's senior year. I was honored to deliver the eulogy at Robby's funeral. Although I was strong during the delivery, I broke down in the last pew of the church after the service was over.

I collected myself, returning to school to teach the rest of the day in first grade. That's what teachers do. That's what

Fred would do. My students needed me as much as I needed them on that difficult day in my life.

Is it just me, or is first grade a unique, extra-special year for students and their families? I think it's a magical year. Most students enter first grade as emergent readers and leave as fluent readers who are ready for anything! The growth in nine months is immeasurable.

I wonder if that was what Robby and his parents appreciated about me. Being the teacher that taught him how to read and write, add and subtract was an unbelievable honor. Being the teacher, they asked to deliver the eulogy for their son was an unforgettable memory… I am crying as I share these words with you.

So, Fred shared in the grieving process with me, even though he didn't know Katlyn or Robby. He used carefully chosen words to express his sympathy. He didn't just send a sympathy card. He called. He wrote a letter. It was meaningful. He was a role model for me to help others with tragedy.

That's what Fred did.

It's important for you to understand that my teaching experience (my life) has been touched by many other hardships, but I have only chosen to highlight a few of the losses. We have lost teachers and I have assisted in their services through song and I will be forever touched by their contributions to our children. Teachers help to shape each other's passion, so when we lose a fellow teacher, we lose a part of our "being." These pivotal moments in the life of an educator are draining, but they remind us of the importance of who we are.

I can recall our principal sharing a "moment of silence" over the intercom during the Morning Announcements after the death of a teacher. Tears streamed down my face in front of my first graders. It's at these moments that children become the caregivers. My students ran to me for a "group hug," knowing that it would bring me comfort. I believe that children are so resilient. They can bring comfort to adults. The "flood gates" are opening as I reflect on this memory.

Do you know that this same day during recess, a rainbow appeared over our school? What made this so significant is that it was a day without rain. Our entire school felt this was "Debbie's Masterpiece" letting us know that she was safe, healed, and happy.

It was a Gift from God. The bond between the teachers in my school was so strong.

When we lose a fellow teacher, we lose a family member.

One last thought about loss (for now) and how we can learn to be a part of the assistance in the transitioning from our Earthly Days to Heaven. There was a time when members of my Chancel Choir at New Wilmington Presbyterian Church were taking turns caring for a loving member of our choir who was dying in a local hospital. She was a single woman in her mid-seventies. She had very little family, so her choir members were her family. We took eight hour "shifts" to sit with her, sing to her, pray with her. Although she could speak, it was difficult to understand what she was trying to communicate, and as the days went on, she became silent, with strained breathing. We would write in a journal that was at the foot of her bed, so the next choir member would be "up to speed" as to what happened during the prior shift. I wrote to Fred about this. His response was:

"What a beautiful person you are! Thank you <u>indeed</u> for sharing something so personal with me. I feel it a privilege to know as much about you as you feel you can trust me with. Your "neighbor" is blessed to have you help her as she makes that important transition…like being born…into a new life. What comfort to be with someone who is so close to Heaven! That's her gift to you right now."

As I have experienced the honor of being with both of my parents as they took their last breath, Fred's words rang true more than ever. My parents taught me so much during their last chapter in life. Thanks, Fred. Loss is a part of life. It helps to shape who we are. It is a privilege to "provide" for our loved ones as they transition to the ultimate place of peace.

Chapter Four

Our Friendships

As time moved forward, I felt our bond continue to grow. In one letter to Fred, I shared my friendship with my college peer, Pete. Pete and I were and are the best of buddies. We were fraternity brothers. I was his best man. He and his wife, Marj, allowed me to be an important part of their child's life from birth all the way up to the latest event, her wedding.

Sarah, their daughter, asked me to read scripture for her wedding that took place at Chautauqua Institution in Chautauqua, New York. (By the way, the institution's bookstore has a wonderful display of Mister Rogers' books and memorabilia…the Fred Rogers display is nestled among political greats like Ruth Bader Ginsburg and artists such as Van Gogh and Bob Ross.)

As I try to share my relationships with people like Pete, I think it is important for me to explain how a particular educational theorist has helped me to understand the significance of deep friendships. Eric Erikson, an educational theorist whom both Fred and I appreciated, was known for developing the Eight Stages of Psychosocial Development. It's in the sixth stage from 20 years to 45 years that Erikson suggests as the time humans most often meet their "life partner." When I teach the Erikson Theory in my Educational Psychology Class, I am quick to inform my college students that I have never met my "life partner," but all of the other stages were met with such great fanfare, that I was able to be happy and successful in life without this stage being completed as Erikson wished.

Pete, was one of those people who allowed me to be a part of his daughter's upbringing, thus helping me to fulfill part of Erikson's theory. Pete and Marj allowed me to visit once a month on weekends. I became Sarah's "babysitter" all weekend long. I spent most of my time with Sarah, playing "restaurant" or "grocery." We watched Mary Poppins every time I visited. We told non-sensical jokes that made us laugh until we cried. I even changed her diaper (not very successfully, but I did it). Although not a blood relative, they assigned me the name of "Uncle Todd" the first day I held Sarah in my arms.

I share this, because I think it's important to know that when your life doesn't "fit" into a regular mold (as a mentioned earlier in a chapter about being alone), there should be loved ones close by to invite you to be a part of their lives so that you can grow and learn through a "stage" like that of Erikson's.

Fred appreciated my thoughts. It inspired him to write about a friendship of his:

"You and Pete must share a very special friendship. It's good that you can have such devoted friends. My friend, Jim, was one of my closest friends from the time we began high school. (I was his best man. My Dad was like a father to him after his own Dad died when we were teenagers.) I went to the hospital every night for a week after work – (those were the days of live television!) when Jim's son Bob was in an automobile accident. At the end of the week Bob died. I visited him in South Carolina (where he was working for Westinghouse) just a week before he died. He had been dealing with cancer several years and grew stronger and stronger in his faith each day! What a privilege to know him! Friendship like that are gifts from God. Writing this to YOU was "good therapy" (as you call it) for ME."

I have a few more special college friends who opened their hearts and families to me. The Ryans, Allstons and Frambes all have children who call me "Uncle Todd." I've been able to be a guest at all of their special events from graduations to weddings.

It's an honor to be an important part of their lives. I marvel at the amazing "parenting work" I witness within the homes of my immediate family and friends. Bravo!

I must also mention my "real" brother, John, who invites me to be a part of his children's lives whenever we can get together. He lives in the beautiful state of Vermont. My brother has adopted his grandson. Although, out of the ordinary, it's more common than you may imagine. Toward the end of my career, there seemed to be at least one family of grandparents as the core make-up of a child's parental unit. My brother, John, is doing a remarkable job. Fred would be so proud of him. I know that Fred would be the first to applaud

John's good work and he would acknowledge that there are all types of families that make our world special.

Hooray for my kind, gentle spirit of a brother! John, you are a masterpiece.

I look forward to the next wedding, the next baby, and the next vacation spent with these special people.

Thank you for being YOU.

Chapter Five

The Gift of Silence

Fred loved silence. It is one of the things I grew to love about Fred. Silence can be uncomfortable to some people when there is a "lull" in the conversation. This wasn't the case with Fred. When he was quiet, he was just allowing us to have time to think. In a letter, I had mentioned how silence gave me moments/hours to be creative.

He replied in a letter, "Obviously, YOU, Todd, recognize the great value of silence. You talked about driving and thinking, taking the time to think! I'm wondering how we can help children discover that important part of their life? How can we help them understand that nourishing their souls through silence is a very important...very deep thing to do!?!?"

It was through his words that I was reminded that "wait time" after asking a question was essential. We need to allow for the process of thinking to happen. His words gave new meaning to the phrase "Silence is golden."

That's what Fred did. He helped me gain a greater appreciation for silence.

When we are silent, we listen. Fred was a great listener. He listened to people. He listened to nature. I have taught my students to listen by taking a "Listening Walk" with me.

We walked with our clipboards and pencil in hand, writing down the various sounds we heard in the classrooms, hallways, offices, and playground. I plan on doing this with my college students this fall.

There are many wonderful children's books about the skill of "listening." When we teach the Five Senses in Science, a Listening Walk can become a Nature Walk if you take the time to venture outside the classroom and into the "real world."

Remember that Listening Walks require no talking. We rely on our ears for this activity. It's neat to reconvene in the classroom to share the different sounds each person heard during the walk. After our discussion, my students write and/or draw something that they heard on our listening walk.

Fred had a great deal of silence in his shows. If you take the time to reflect on his use of silence within each show, I think you will be amazed as to how many seconds of silence between delicate piano and dialogue are incorporated within episodes of The Neighborhood. Fred shared with me that he did this deliberately, so children had time to process their thoughts…time to think.

Recently, I was asked to make a short video that would be shared with my last class of fourth graders who graduated from high school in 2025. I was honored that they would remember me. (I thought that since I had not been teaching in the district for eight years, they would have forgotten about Old Mr. Cole.) When I viewed my self-made video before sending it to the Senior Class, I found myself pausing between thoughts on the video. It must have been something I had intentionally or unintentionally learned along the way from Fred that I have embedded as part of my delivery of thoughtful information with students. Silence can be very powerful, for it allows us time to reflect and make sense of our feelings. I hope my graduates sensed the connection that I was trying to make with them. As my "last class," they were very special to me.

I attended their graduation ceremony at Laurel High School, as I have for all of my past classes, and was surprised that I was a focal point of William's speech, who was 2025's Salutatorian. Sometimes, you don't realize the difference you make in the lives of children. His words brought me to tears.

Fred believed in expressing feelings, in an appropriate way. Crying is a way we express love, sorrow, even joy. In my opinion, he was the first and the best at teaching our children how to deal with feelings.

Feeling mad or sad are very deep and complex emotions that children need to learn how to navigate. Fred was an expert in helping children cope with their feelings.

A true gift.

Chapter Six

The Ocean

We shared an appreciation for the ocean. Fred once sent me a feather from a bird he found while walking on the beach in Florida. He placed the feather in an envelope and on the back of the envelope he wrote: "T. found this feather this morning. It wants to be with you. F."

What would Fred do? Fred modeled an appreciation for nature and shared "simple, yet very important gifts" with the people he loved. The feather is one of my most treasured gifts. He, as he always did, taught me the love for nature and for writing letters as a form of deep communication.

Fred would also write to me from his summer home in Nantucket. He had stationery with a drawing of the cottage on the front, labeled 'The Crooked House-Nantucket.' Apparently, it truly was "crooked." If you "Google' images of Fred, you will find several photos of him walking the beach and watching the waves in silence.

I worked at my parents' business for 19 summers in Wells Beach, Maine. It was a "Ma and Pa" cottage and motel establishment. Prior to purchasing the business, our family had vacationed in York Beach, Maine every summer when I was a child. Jumping over and diving into the cold waves of the Atlantic are some of my fondest memories as a child. (The ocean water of Maine was quite cold, but that was part of the initial jolt that I grew to appreciate.)

I continue to vacation in Maine every month of June with my golden retriever. It is my place to rejuvenate and just walk the beach with my dog, Titan. I visit all of our family's favorite places to eat. I attend my parents' church and worship from the back row. I particularly love to catch the sunrise. It's a slice of heaven. How can one not appreciate this gift of nature?

Here is a "P.S." from one of Fred's letters to me:

"Isn't it great to have 'memory.' We can think about the seashore even when we're not there! F."

At one point in our written communication, I must have sent Fred a scenic card of the ocean. His opening remarks from his next letter:

"Dear Todd,

Thanks so much for the beautiful card. (You know how much I love waves!)"

Another correspondence from a postcard:

"We're in Nantucket until 7/9 then back to Pittsburgh. It is GORGEOUS here. Swimming every afternoon in front of the house."

Fred was a swimmer. He swam every morning at an indoor pool in Pittsburgh. He prayed while he swam. He told me of this during one of our conversations. This form of exercise helped him to stay at a slim 143 pounds…so disciplined. I have that number (143) on my office door at Westminster, for it represents the letters in "I love you."

The cover of this book expresses our desire to gaze into the majesty of the sunrise of the ocean. It expresses hope. The waves are endless, just as our affection for making life a better place for our children.

Chapter Seven

Bullies

Fred and I shared our love for our own teachers, particularly our elementary teachers. They were instrumental in guiding us in the direction to our calling. Our parents, being our first teachers, were the foundation of it all. However, our teachers and parents didn't always see what happened outside of our home or classroom walls.

Bullies were another common link we shared. We were both bullied as children. Neither of us spoke of it to each other. I read about Fred's incidents as a child and his ability to rise above it. He was overweight in his youth and was chased home from school by unkind peers. Laura Renauld, who wrote the children's book, *Fred's Big Feelings: The Life and Legacy of Mister Rogers* with illustrations by Brigette Barrager, published by Athenaeum Books, shared this event within the text.

Even though our childhood obstacles were "unspoken topics," I believe the "unspoken" was a thread that weaved a deep connection between us. When I reflect on my upbringing, I think my kindness was mistaken for weakness. I was so gentle and naïve, and perhaps Fred was, too. I think those qualities can be "uncomfortable" for some peers at the middle-school age. Perhaps bullying was the only way they knew how to deal with it?

As adults, Fred and I weren't afraid to show the "sensitive" side of our personalities. As teachers of young children, our delivery was often gentle. Fred would often end a phone conversation or phone message with the words, "Bye bye, my dear." I can honestly say that I don't ever recall any other person closing a conversation with those words. Yet, I would use "dear" as a form of affection toward my students.

I think we tend to end those words of affection when we become adults…particularly as men. Fred's words were honest and sincere. He considered me to be "dear." I believe it to be endearing…a synonym for "fond." Please don't confuse Fred's sensitivity with being feminine. Fred was someone who was comfortable in his own skin. This made him one of the most masculine men I knew. I wish more men were as sensitive as Fred.

I wonder what our world would be like if men were less afraid to show their feelings.

That's what Fred did.

I believe Fred and I had a "constant." It was our family and faith. Family and faith helped us deal with the name calling and the hardship of unkind acts. I also think it assisted us as adults to form our mission to help young children appreciate who they were, and hopefully prevent some of the bullying that happened to us.

For me the most difficult time of bullying was when my family moved to Connecticut in the middle of my sixth-grade year. I was leaving a self-contained classroom in New Jersey and moving into a departmentalized program where I had several teachers and a locker with a pad lock. It was so foreign to me. Although I had been teased in my past school, I had no idea what was in store for me as a skinny, short, very naive sixth-grader. In the spring of sixth grade, two classmates who rode the same bus as me, wrote the words, "F….t Go Home Go Away" with shaving cream all over the side of our house. I will never forget my dad holding my mom in his arms as she cried looking at the message that was clearly meant for me. At that time, I thought "the f word" meant that I wore "white socks."

I was extremely sheltered. I could share many more embarrassing stories regarding my "innocence," but that would be an entirely different book. Moving on, I knew the word was an insult. My parents tried to speak to me about it, but I didn't want to call attention to it. The words had been washed away from the side of our home, so I thought I should wipe them from my mind. Our family really never forced me to address it head on. Instead, we dove into "family and church life" to heal the wounds.

As an adult, I look back and wonder if we would have handled it differently if it had happened in today's world that provided children's books about bullying and when talking about it in therapy was more "accepted."

There is a wealth of anti-bully programs and resources that weren't available in the 1970s. I encourage you to seek for these types of books if an occasion should arise that lends itself to helping a child work through difficult situations such as bullying.

More difficult situations happened as I entered high school. I remember as a freshman in high school I had my head shoved in my locker by a football player. Another time, I was tossed in the showers, fully clothed, after gym class. I recall running home after school, through the woods (shortcut), so that I would arrive home before my mother got home from work (she was our church secretary) in order to put my clothes in the dryer. I wanted to "hide" the event from my family.

Eventually, as time went on, I was a bit more accepted, as was Fred. Fred was elected President of his senior class. I was elected Treasurer of Student Government, and I was voted to be an escort for Homecoming Court. So, I guess someone liked me, but it was definitely a tough time for me. I'm hoping those who bullied me have grown up to be better humans.

And to be fair, I did my share of name-calling. I think because I was bullied so badly, I chose one girl to tease. I think I had a crush on her and teasing was my inappropriate way of getting her attention. I wish I could apologize to her. I tried finding her on social media, but no luck. I believe childhood experiences can be difficult, but if we have a "faithful family foundation of love", it can make a huge difference.

So, what did Fred do? What did Todd do? I think we both chose to use our experiences of unkind treatment and turned them into something good for the future. I believe that Fred and I used the events from our past to help create a brighter future for our children by focusing on how to teach children to treat one another.

Fred was the "King of Kindness." I have tried to model kindness, knowing that I have failed, miserably at times. However, I never lost sight of the goal to be the best I could be for our children. As far as Fred and I are concerned, I believe our trials and tribulations as students made us the humans we became in our separate, yet same, ministries in education. I call them ministries, for I know Fred called his show a "television ministry."

As I mentioned earlier, I decided to devote my life to teaching children, so I consider it my ministry, too.

I have shared my childhood "bullying" experiences with every group of college students. As I looked out at them while sharing the stories, I saw tears, I saw shock. I wanted them to know that I turned out to be a successful member of society, and I hoped the "bullies" did, too.

Sharing my unkind experiences shines a light on WHY my message of "kindness" is so crucial. Sharing my personal walk with unkind peers, brings us together as humans and it makes my teaching more meaningful. It teaches empathy. It allows my college students to be "seen and heard," for I imagine many of them have suffered at the hands and/or words of bullies.

Speaking of empathy, do you remember when Fred did a segment on "dying?" I spoke to Fred about that segment. He found a dead fish in the tank, and he buried it outside the Neighborhood Home. As he buried the fish, he shared the loss of his dog when he was a child and how it made him feel. At that moment the viewers, young and old, felt close to Fred. I'm sure they had similar experiences and it helped to form a bond between Fred and his television neighbors.

It didn't just teach sympathy, but it taught empathy. Fred could tackle tough topics on an appropriate level for young children. He modeled it for all adults so that the issues were not taboo in their homes. Fred made it easier for parents to discuss heavy subject matter.

I have a postcard that Fred sent to me from Winter Park Florida with a picture of Rollins College (his alma mater). I had sent a letter to him about the death of one of our family dogs, Shadow.

His response: "I'll always remember having to take our 21-year-old cat to the Vet who helped her go to Heaven. I stayed right with her. Know that you're in my warmest thoughts. You too are a masterpiece."

Chapter Eight

9/11

We all remember Fred's advice during his Public Service Announcement after 9/11. "Look for the helpers." Everyone was looking for wisdom; for a way to make sense of something so unbelievable. Fred managed to look and listen to his surroundings from the newscasts of the day, and he saw and heard people helping one another in their time of need. We couldn't change what happened in our world on 9/11, but Fred helped us move forward with the knowledge of people helping people…a very Godly thing to do.

His family taught him to "look for the helpers" and he was passing this knowledge onto us.

It was on that horrific day at Laurel Elementary that I first asked "What would Fred do?" Again, very few teachers had technology on their phones that could share what was happening. We would get "bits and pieces" from the principal's office through email and a stern warning to refrain from turning on our classroom televisions. Slowly, but surely, teachers were getting messages from their husbands, wives, and parents acknowledging the horrific events. First one building, then another, then the Pentagon and the field in Somerset County, Pennsylvania. I did receive a phone message from a parent of one of my students requesting that I tell her son that it was OK to pray.

I was at a loss as to how I should address the national news with my first-graders or if at all, but when I thought of Fred, it became clear. I knew he'd want me to make it age-appropriate. So, at the end of the day, I asked all of my students to join hands with me in a circle. It was then that I told my Class of Masterpieces that something bad happened in our world, today.

I told them that their parents would tell them about it when they got home, but all they needed to know right now was that this circle would never be broken and that I would always be here to protect them. I think my words were meant just as much for me as they were for my students.

Children need to know that the classroom is a Safe Haven for them. If they don't feel safe in their surroundings, they won't feel comfortable to learn…to take risks…to fail…to achieve…to cry…to laugh…to share...to love.

Fred was pleased with how I handled it when I shared it with him in a later conversation. I thanked him for his words that still ring true to this day. Whenever something horrific happens in our world, there is always a newscaster that refers to Fred's advice…Look for the helpers.

Chapter Nine

A Great Loss

On January 1, 2003, I saw Fred on the television riding in a convertible for The Rose Parade as Grand Marshall. I was unaware of Fred's participation until I saw it on the television. I later learned that Fred was very ill. He had an aggressive form of stomach cancer. Fred died, less than two months later, on February 27, 2003. I joined in the sorrow with all Americans.

In the grand scheme of things, he wasn't very old. He was 74 years young. I was devastated. What would I do without him? No more letters. No more meetings. More importantly, what would children do without him?

Children and adults looked to him for guidance. He was our "faith-filled compass" through his television ministry and his meaningful messages he shared after he ended the tapings of his "neighborhood."

I received an invitation to his Memorial Service that was held in Pittsburgh. I was sent two tickets. I invited my friend,

Ellen, who shared in my loss and was instrumental in touching my life through Fred. As we walked a few blocks from our parking garage to the auditorium, we had to pass a group of silent protesters. I didn't understand the significance, but Ellen did. Ellen grabbed my arm and told me to keep on walking.

My friend shared that she thought it was a group who traveled the country to protest outside of funerals of people who fought for ideals that went against their beliefs. Ellen's explanation was difficult to grasp. Knowing everyone has a right to peacefully protest, it was troublesome. I was grieving. How could Fred, everyone's "neighbor", be seen as someone other than a loving example for humanity? But, again, it was their right. Confusing thoughts quickly changed, for the moment we opened the lobby doors to the theater, we were greeted with floor to ceiling letters and artwork from children all around the world.

It was heartwarming.

Children's thoughts: "Thank you for teaching me to be kind." I am certain that Fred would have been pleased that the lobby focused on the messages from children. After the service, I had the chance to thank Joanne Rogers for sharing Fred with all of us. I had met her only a few times when I went to her piano recitals that she and her friend, Jeannine, performed on the campus of my alma mater, Westminster College. I also met her at a Book Release Party for a biography written by Max King that took place in the Children's History Museum of Pittsburgh.

Fred's Memorial was an inspiring service with some of his favorite guests from "the neighborhood" like Yo-Yo Ma. It was filled with music which is what Fred would have wanted. Fred certainly was a talented musician. He wrote all the music (lyrics/melodies) for every production of "Mister Rogers' Neighborhood." The Memorial Service was a form of healing for me. I was grateful that Ellen, who helped initiate our friendship, could be with me at the closing of my earthly contact with Fred.

Thank you, Ellen. I am forever grateful.

After Fred died, life continued to "happen." I found myself wishing that Fred was still alive for support during life-changing events.

My parents eventually moved to be close to me in New Wilmington, Pa. They joined my church. They relished in being a part of my life as an educator. My dad died after Fred had reached his Day of Glory.

After Dad died, I came to realize that Fred and my dad were working together as Angels on a mission to help me continue as an educator for children.

I am certain my dad was guiding my mother as she spent every day with me as I recovered from cancer in a "long-term hospital." He gave her the strength to be strong for me…reading prayers and scripture to me when I could hear but couldn't concentrate to read due to all my meds. I know both Fred and my dad were working as angels to help others to help my mom to stay strong during those difficult months by providing rides for her to stay by my side all day, every day, in a hospital that was too far for her to commute on her own as an 80-year-old woman. I applaud my mom's faithful strength that she modeled for everyone when visitors came to visit me. She was steadfast, but it was clear she had a "higher support system."

When I was cured, I became the caregiver for my mom as she was dealt a form of cancer that was terminal. I know my dad and Fred (and other family members who had "half left" us) were working through my family, friends, colleagues, and church members as they supported me to be strong for my mom as her provider. I loved reading prayers and singing to her at least four times a day as a ritual that paved the way to her Day of Glory.

During Mom's illness, she was confined to a hospital bed in our sunroom. My neighbor shopped for my mom so that I had something to "open on Christmas Day." They made a list together, so that Mom could be part of the process of trying to make the holiday special. Just being by my mom's side was the greatest gift she could have given me, but I appreciated the joy it brought her to see me open gifts that Maggie, our neighbor, purchased on Mom's behalf.

Pete, my best friend who I mentioned in an earlier chapter, visited every night after work. He sat next to my mom and me on cold dark winter nights in the sunroom as we shared good memories together. This was so therapeutic for all of us. I am certain that my church members and people across the country on prayer chains were there when my brother traveled countless times from Vermont. Their prayers kept my brother safe as he traveled from New England. It was clear that angels and those living among us were helping me to be strong. What a gift it is for me to reflect on this sacred time and be able to see God at work through his Heavenly and Earthly Angels!

So even though Fred wasn't "living" when my dad died, when I lived through cancer, and when my mom died, he WAS there…he was working "in concert" with many others. I believe that it is those who have gone before us that guide us in our journey to become better people.

Sometimes I have a conversation with them to discuss a problem or to give gratitude to them.

Chapter Ten

Reconnecting

After my mom's death, I was struggling to revamp my "purpose." I lived with my mom. When she was given the diagnosis of terminal cancer, our bond grew closer than ever. Hospice came for an hour, two or three times a week and I had 14 hours a week of outside services to sit with Mom while I taught college students. The rest of the time, Mom and I spent every hour talking, watching Hallmark and Jeopardy, praying, singing and sleeping. I was able to do my school work while Mom rested. My recliner (my makeshift bed) would be placed against the side of Mom's hospital bed in our sunroom. Often, I would reach for her hand in the dark of night and tap it three times (one tap for each word in the phrase "I love you"). She would always tap back, three times.

When she died, the home was extremely quiet and there was no more "tapping." We had lost our family dog during mom's battle, so the silence of being the only living family member in the house was deafening.

One person, who watched from afar, knew that my "first Christmas" without Mom would be hard. His name was Rev. Jim Mohr. He was/is the Chaplin of Westminster College. His daughter was in charge of an annual Holiday Parade in a neighboring town. Jim, had made contact with one of his "neighbors" to be the Grand Marshall for the parade. His name was David Newell, aka Mr. McFeely.

Jim had asked if I would be willing to pick David Newell up from the hotel to bring him to the parade route. Of course, I replied with a joyful "YES!" Jim had already established a close friendship with David, and I sense that Jim knew I needed my spirits to be lifted.

This was a huge jolt! I had the opportunity to reacquaint myself with David and share "Fred Stories" with him as I drove him to the parade line up. I was able to present him with a copy of my children's book *You Are a Masterpiece!*

Prior to the parade, I had made signs that my college students, colleagues, and current fraternity brothers could hold as they walked down Main Street. My friend, Pete, organized the fraternity brothers to carry the signs.

I constructed a banner, carried by my college students, that stated, "Westminster College Thanks YOU For Being Their Neighbor!" I stayed with David, who was in full Mr. McFeely attire, throughout the evening as he sat in the cold beside the town's Christmas Tree, signing autographs for a line of fans.

It's worth noting that the tree for the town's parade that year was donated by one of my past student's families. It was a tree that I gave Trevor thirty years ago from a seedling on Earth Day in first grade. It had grown to an enormous size and was perfectly shaped and adorned with bright, colored lights. Needless to say, my heart was full that evening, and I believe that God was working extra hard for me through Jim Mohr, David McFeely, Trevor's Family, my college colleagues, students, friends, and fraternity.

The stars were aligned that special night!

While my mom approached her "Earthly Death," she made me promise that I would get another golden retriever when the time was right, because she knew I would be lonely. I shared this in a letter with David (Mr. McFeely) when I had made the decision to open my heart to another four-legged family member. His response:

"A golden retriever!! You must like active dogs…we have a 200-pound English Mastiff and he, "Bear," is a couch potato! Lovely dog…eats like a horse!"

I had asked his opinion on a name for my golden. I had narrowed it down to two names, Titan (the mascot for Westminster College) or Dyson (as in the vacuum cleaner due to all the shedding of golden retriever hair). David's response:

"I think I like Titan since it relates to WC and the area where you live…although Dyson is funnier! Let me know what you decide…I bet you can't wait." (I was waiting for my pup's magical "eight- week" separation from his mother.) TITAN was the overwhelming vote from most of family and friends, so TITAN it was!

On another occasion, I had the honor of sharing time with David when he spoke at a service in the chapel at Westminster. He came on his 80th birthday! Rev. Jim Mohr, asked me to order a cake to honor his birthday. I had the privilege of bringing it into the chapel with candles lit and a crowd of "neighbors" singing, HAPPY BIRTHDAY!

I think Fred was/is pleased that I had reconnected with David. He's looking down and smiling. It's through these events with David that Jim Mohr helped me realize that with every ending, there is a new beginning. My reestablished connection with David McFeely is still alive and well. You'll see how David/Mr. McFeely helped more lives in my community in a later chapter.

I met David, again, on Cardigan Day in November when it was celebrated at WQED. This was an event that enabled all who loved Fred to gather in one place…what a gift! I went with my Pittsburgh friend, Ellen, who knew more about driving in Pittsburgh than me. (To be honest, almost anyone knows more about driving in a city than me.} I met a new "neighbor", Chris, who had traveled all the way from Connecticut just to be in the presence of Fred's spirit. This is a true testament to Fred's extended influence. Chris was/is a principal at a Christian School in Connecticut. I remember removing my Trolley Pin that I was wearing that night from my red cardigan and giving it to Chris. We are still in contact through texting on holidays and special occasions that remind us of Fred and the Neighborhood.

Isn't it nice to meet new neighbors who share a love for Fred? What a great way to unite in a hope for tomorrow and a mission to make tomorrow a better world for our children! Truly, it was a magical night filled with joy.

My reconnecting with David would never have happened if it weren't for Rev. Jim Mohr. He is a man working as a servant of God.

Chapter Eleven

Faith

We both had a strong faith, and yet we never showcased our religion on television or in the classroom. By "showcasing our religion," I mean that we didn't recite scripture for the television neighbors or students in the classroom. I believe we viewed Fred's faith every time we saw him on Mister Rogers Neighborhood, and yet he never mentioned religion on air. It was his kind words, pleasant expressions, and caring thoughts that developed a connection with his viewers.

As a teacher, it was my mission to establish that same connection with my students that could grow throughout the year in order to make the curriculum come alive; remembering that we don't teach the curriculum. We teach children. Without the connection between Fred and his viewers, and mine with my students, the message could be lost.

So, just like Fred, I hope my students witnessed my faith by playing with the lonely student on the playground or sitting next to the student in class who had a daily stench from dirty clothes. Perhaps they saw my faith in the simple stroke of the chalk on the blackboard and colorful bulletin board displays. Perhaps they saw my faith when I attended their athletic and/or musical events outside of the school day. And maybe, just maybe, they saw my faith when I used my Personal Day to "Read on the School Roof" all day long…showing that reading can happen anywhere… even on a school rooftop.

I think it is undeniable to not see both of our "faiths in play" with our daily work on the television and in the classroom. I think another connection we had was that we were both Presbyterian.

Like Fred, they may have seen my faith in our daily routine of a schedule written on the chalkboard and the positioning of my body at the door every morning as they entered the classroom. Fred had a routine…same beginning and ending of the show, same feeding of the fish. Routine is a "safety net" or "a favorite blanket" that students appreciate at any age. We both modeled it.

I recently visited my parents' home church in Maine while vacationing with Titan. The church, small in physical footage, was large in love for one another and the Lord. The minister concluded with the message of creating a "safe place" for everyone to feel welcomed and loved. He shared the importance of being a servant and being someone of character, for character provides hope.

I spoke with him after the service to thank him for his words and to tell him that his delivery reminded me of Fred

(his cadence and pausing between sentences to allow us to think and soak in his words.)

He immediately said, "Thank you." His response was so quick as to affirm he knew exactly what I was trying to share. He knew what I meant and he found it to be a true compliment.

Then, he proceeded to tell me that he had met "Officer Clemmons." My response was that Fred was way ahead of his time in regard to welcoming people of all colors into his neighborhood.

Do you remember how Fred shared a small pool of water to soak his feet alongside Officer Clemmons? Fred also dried the feet of Francois Clemmons (aka Officer Clemmons). Pastor Greg agreed. I wish we could have continued the conversation. Maybe someday we will. My point of bringing up my visit to this church is to remind us all that Fred truly wished for a world where people were accepted and loved for who they were…providing that "safe place" to land. Pastor Greg was sharing Fred's message, God's message.

I believe it is important to create "safe places" for ALL children (all races, genders, sexual identities, religious beliefs) in public schools. This is a hot topic that has caused many challenges among my Social Media friends. It has caused a few to question my faith…taking issue with what I believe. At times it is hurtful, but just as I stand up for my beliefs, they do, too. Different opinions should be encouraged as long as they aren't expressed with the purpose to hurt others.

Every generation has had social challenges such as Civil Rights, Voting, Aids, Same Sex Marriage, and Transgender, just to name a few. Unfortunately, it seems that all social issues have been mixed in a blender at high speed during the 2020 decade.

I guess what I'm trying to say is that our faith is something that can be measured by how we treat one another. Our faith can be shared by kind words. When we are kind, I believe we are faithful servants. I believe in the Separation of Church and State.

However, I do believe in a "moment of silence". This allows for students to take time to pray or think a "happy thought" ... allowing all children to practice their own faith, not a chosen faith of a school district.

Again, silence is a time that gives us the power to think, to pray, or just create a moment of mindfulness.

Have you ever heard of the Alphabet Prayer? Sometimes when we can't find the words to express our thoughts in prayer. Just sing the Alphabet Song. Every letter in the alphabet is in every word that you are looking for when you are at a loss for how to express it.

I think we should be more vocal when we see God at work in our lives and point it out to others. Fred did this all the time. Fred applauded God's Handy Work in our lives just by letting his television neighbors know that he liked them just the way they were...he was sharing God's thoughts with the children on the other side of the screen.

Fred did it without needing to focus on God's name on his show, but glorifying Him by his thoughts and actions. I believe when we share that message, we share God's Story, not our story. We should be helping one another to make our neighborhoods a more loving place to live. We should sacrifice for our neighbors, and we shouldn't do it to impress, but rather to be worthy. My pastor at New Wilmington Presbyterian Church always challenges us to reach beyond our church walls to help our neighborhood. Thanks, Pastor Matt. (By the way, Matt has a fondness for Fred, too.)

Before my feet hit the ground next to my bed every morning, I quietly say, "Father Use Me." It's simple. I want to be used to better the world around me. I hope my explanation of my faith has helped you to understand how I operate in a world that often seems to be on "life support."

Do I get weary? Absolutely. I count on people around me and my faith to lean on during difficult times.

It's worth noting that I teach on the third floor of Old Main, which is the tallest building on campus...closest place to Heaven at Westminster College. To me, it's a reminder that "Educators are Heaven-sent" and we are being guided in our profession by the greatest teacher of all.

Chapter Twelve

What would Fred want US to do? WWFWUTD?

Everyone, including me, has said, "We sure could use Mister Rogers right now." The world is getting more difficult to navigate on a daily basis. We have a job to do. Fred is telling me that I need to carry his light. Fred would be too humble to call it "his light," but more likely "God's light." I believe it's all of our responsibility to carry his or His vision, his or His message.

I'd like to organize this chapter by assigning a number to each event of how we have started to share Fred's Light.

1.

When the Massacre of Sandy Hook Elementary happened on December 14, 2012, we were all looking for answers from someone else. It's OUR job to make a change for the better. We can do it, peacefully. I did it by writing an editorial about visiting the Memorial of Sandy Hook. I did it by letting my loved ones know that instead of Christmas Gifts, I would be sending a donation in their name to Sandy Hook Promise, a non-profit organization that sponsors legislation for more mental health funding and common-sense gun reform.

It's difficult to "stay afloat" when these shootings occur. Every time there is a school shooting, I almost become paralyzed. But then I remember, "Look for the helpers!" I saw many running to the aid of the school and local hospitals. I also found myself encouraging my Facebook friends to give to a non-profit organization like Sandy Hook Promise and also share children's books that help children in the aftermath of school shootings.

We need to be part of the solution.

2.

In May of 2025, I was interviewed on our college's cable television station by a Broadcasting Major, Benjamin Kelly. Much of our "talk" that was to focus on the upcoming Rotary event, Peace in the Park, took a turn to have a conversation about Fred and our connection with "peace." Benjamin noted in our interview that through our email correspondences in preparation for the interview I always ended my emails with, "Peace, Mr. Cole."

He asked me why I did that. I shared with Benjamin that I started ending every letter to my fourth graders, parents, and colleagues with the word "peace" after the Sandy Hook Shooting. It really changed me. Our discussion about Peace and Fred seemed to be meaningful to Benjamin. Here was his thoughtful email he sent to me after our interview:

"I hope you enjoyed your time on the Titan Radio Roundtable. It was such a joy to engage in that conversation with you. Rarely does an interview stay with me for two weeks afterward. However, I found myself so moved by your words and ideology towards others that I have almost felt lighter in the weeks following. Looking for the helpers and the best in peers and professionals.

Thank you for your courtesy and kindness during the interview. I would love to connect with you again soon.

Peace,

Benjamin Kelly"

This is another example of how writing a letter or email to express your thoughts can be so meaningful. Benjamin, as a college student, was going beyond the responsibility of a campus news anchor.

Be like Fred and Be like Benjamin.

3.

After my mother died, my colleagues from Laurel Elementary, and Westminster College, along with church members, gathered on the chapel steps with luminaries that spelled the word "PEACE." I was so touched. THAT'S what Fred would want us to do. He would want us to help each other through the struggles of life.

Be there for your loved ones. Put the cell phone down and connect with them face to face. What my chosen family did for me that night took so much preparation with Rev. Mohr, my faculty at WC and Laurel, Mom's friends, and best friends like Pete and Marj. They had worked all day, and they were willing to gather to support me on a very cold night.

Be like all of them.

4.

After The Tree of Life Massacre in Pittsburgh, Fred had already reached his Day of Glory, but his wife Joanne and Tom Hanks (who was in town for the filming of a Mister Rogers' movie) both had words of comfort to share at a Peace Rally after the synagogue shooting.

Joanne said, "Let us replace guns with hugs." (Facebook, KDKA-TV, Pittsburgh, Nov. 8, 2018) I believe that Fred would have shared a similar message. Her statement addressed both gun reform and mental health at the same time. That's what Fred would have done. I had my college students in my Educational Psychology Class create a Tree of Life with their names on the leaves of the tree to display in our classroom. Creating art can be a way of addressing sorrow or allowing us to acknowledge an event in a meaningful, personal way.

Be like Joanne…give hugs.

5.

Another avenue that I have traveled to shine Fred's light is by sharing a video, *Our Assignment from Fred Rogers,* produced by high school students of the Fox Chapel School District, with my college students in my Educational Psychology Class. It shares interviews from preschoolers, Fred's staff and on-air actors, Joanne, his children, and Max King, the author of the biography, *The Good Neighbor: The Life and Work of Fred Rogers*. In a nutshell, this gave a beautiful insight to how Fred created a special place for young children, along with their families, to experience ways to navigate through times of trouble and celebrate times of joy. It opened the door to Fred's loving staff and how they saw the workings of Fred in "real time." This documentary, which can be found on You Tube, was extremely influential this past semester. I had an exchange student from Costa Rica visiting for one semester who had never heard of Mister Rogers. It was through my stories and this video/documentary that this student developed a true love for Fred's television ministry.

On the last day of class, my student presented me with a drawing she had created of Fred and Daniel the Tiger. Needless to say, tears flowed. It was such a meaningful, kind gesture from a young woman whom I most likely will never see again. I have framed her drawing, and it is part of my personal "Mister Rogers' Museum." I thank Ryan Devlin, from the Fox Chapel School District, for allowing me to share this documentary with you.

Be like the students of Fox Chapel with Ryan Devlin as their advisor.

Be like Estefanny from Costa Rica. Go the extra mile.

6.

I have a fond memory of a local Television Morning News Anchor, Mike Case, who televised a segment from my house many years after Fred passed away. We sat in my living room and we "just talked" about Fred. I shared letters. I shared moments that I have discussed with you in this book.

When the segment was aired, Mike's co-anchor was teary-eyed. Her emotions were raw.

Memories of Fred are held dear by everyone and sometimes our love of Mister Rogers triggers an emotion. I believe my talk with Mike Case brought all the viewers to a place in their own childhood that flooded them with memories of a more innocent time. Fred's message was so simple, yet profound.

Be kind.

Mike's expertise in his field of broadcasting helped to paint a picture for the viewers; enabling them to take a moment before they started their day to be a part of something special. Mike gave the viewer "permission" to pause during their busy morning to reenter their own childhood. Mike Case and I are still good friends, and I appreciate his talent for capturing what Fred meant to me during that segment. This was Mike's way of sharing Fred with our neighborhood. Mike helped adult viewers to connect with each other by reflecting on their own love for Fred.

I'd like to think that the segment assisted viewers to contemplate how they could celebrate everyone's unique contribution to society; challenging viewers to be a part of the solution by being better neighbors for one another.

Be like Mike.

7.

I have a fellow educator, who now teaches first-graders in Room 106 at Laurel Elementary…the same room where I had taught first-graders, so many years ago. Her name is Stephanie Hennon.

She has answered the question, "What would Fred want us to do?" Stephanie orchestrated a week-long theme of "Won't You Be My Neighbor?" in conjunction with Cardigan Day on November 13th and the upcoming film starring Tom Hanks as Fred Rogers.

She told me that we have a Dr. Seuss Week in the month of March, so why not have a Mister Rogers Week in November? Stephanie went as far as calling the Transit Authority of New Castle to ask if they would be willing to deliver a trolley to Laurel Elementary School to be used as the Story Time Venue with me as the storyteller.

Well, who wouldn't do something special in honor of Fred? The Transit Authority "delivered!" One might say it was a "Special Delivery." It provided a perfect "setting" for my story telling about Mister Rogers.

I decorated the inside of the trolley with phrases, "Welcome to the Neighborhood!" and "You are special!" The trolley was a unique setting that provided a special memory for kids who were eager to learn about their Television Neighbor.

Stephanie asked all of the teachers to decorate their hallway bulletin boards in honor of Fred. Wow! You should have seen the creativity! They were amazing! Stephanie was spreading Fred's light to another generation. She proved that he is still with us in spirit and his message is alive and well.

Thanks, Stephanie. You are a masterpiece!

Be like Stephanie.

8.

Introducing Ms. Tracy Andrews and Dr. Jennifer Toney, who have shined a light on Fred's mission in a very special way! They introduced me to a yearly "frED Camp" that supplies teachers to learn new techniques/strategies that develop questioning, curiosity, and a love for learning. The entire day has an underlying theme of Fred's spirit. REMAKE

LEARNING, a non-profit organization is the sponsor of the yearly workshop. Over 200 teachers gather on a Saturday morning in May to learn, share ideas, and just relish in their common love for Fred Rogers. Truly, it is a special day for everyone who attends.

This past year, the workshop was held at The Fred Rogers Institute in Fred's hometown of Latrobe, Pennsylvania. If you ever have the opportunity to visit this museum, it will be worth the trip.

Tracy and Jennifer also spear headed an annual event at our school district's football field called "Reading Under the Lights!" I had the opportunity to read *Mister Rogers' Gift of Music,* written by Donna Cangelosi with illustrations by Amanda Calatzis, to children who came to celebrate reading under the football stadium of lights on a crisp, Fall night. The author writes of how Fred would play (and often bang) on the piano when he wanted to relieve his emotions of anger. So, after I finished reading this marvelous story to children, I placed five keyboards on the green turf of the football field. I allowed the kids to "bang" on the keys to imitate and remember how Mister Rogers dealt with his feelings of anger, eventually turning into something melodic and peaceful after surrendering his anger to more happy thoughts.

As I mentioned earlier, music was an essential part of Fred's life. He used it as a tool to help him deal with a spectrum of emotions and it became an integral part of his Neighborhood television segments. If you have a chance to "relive" his shows, you'll observe how music took "center stage" when he featured guest musicians. For me, I found his use of music to be most meaningful when it was a replacement for dialogue. Just a few notes from the piano while Fred fed the fish could help the "chore" seem whimsical…playful.

"Thank you" to Tracy and Jennifer for being masters in the Field of Education. These two teachers are doing what Fred would want them to do.

Be like Tracy and Jennifer.

9.

I enjoy being a volunteer/guest reader for our church Preschool. Oh, how I enjoy seeing the youngest of minds sparkle through facial expressions as I turn one page to the next in a book that inspires them to become readers. It is a privilege. Plus, I can't express the gratitude I have for Mollie and Julie who are the teacher and assistant for our preschoolers. They work so hard with patience and love. They aren't paid enough for the "calling" they have so willingly embraced. They are the first "official teachers" for children, academically, socially, and emotionally. I use the word "official," because we all know that every parent is a child's "first teacher."

Be like Mollie and Julie, and consider volunteering to read for young minds.

10.

I had a yearning to create a special way to show PEACE in our community. Many of Fred's Christmas Cards had a message of PEACE. One of the cards had white doves and PEACE written in six different languages…it was a card sponsored by UNICEF.

He would often end his letters to me by signing, "Grace and Peace, Fred" or "Shalom, Fred." With my mission to create a peace event, I used my membership as a Rotarian in the New Wilmington Rotary Club to launch PEACE IN THE PARK DAY. Thanks to Rev. Jim Mohr, a fellow Rotarian, David Newell, aka Mr. McFeeley, visited PEACE IN THE PARK DAY as our special guest.

The line of adults with their children to meet David was long, but worth the wait. As I spoke with his fans, patiently waiting, the discussion wasn't about needing to get home or to the Little League Baseball Field. It was about their memories of Fred. Waiting in line was a privilege as everyone shared stories about their favorite episodes and how the show helped them deal with their own feelings. David spent time with each family. He was sincere and authentic, just like Fred.

David is a masterpiece.

Be like David.

We had college students from The School of Education at Westminster College provide arts and crafts with themes of peace for children to create. We had local children's book authors talk to children and present their books.

We had story time for toddlers, and sponsored art classes for kids. Music was provided by the School of Broadcasting students and Titan Radio. A food truck with Haitian Food was offered to our guests. We had a Parade of Flags from Around the World as we all sang "Let There Be Peace on Earth" composed by the songwriting team of Sy Miller and Jill Jackson Miller.

This year our Rotary Club planted a ROTARY INTERNATIONAL PEACE POLE in our Community Park. It has "May Peace Prevail on Earth" written in eight different languages on the four sides of the pole. Leaders in our town shared quotes/poems/thoughts/prayers that explained what "peace" meant to them.

I shared a thought about Peace that Fred once shared. He talked about how we can still be at war with ourselves and each other even if we are not at battle with another country though military force. In other words, we can be at war in our homes, schools, communities, states, and country.

It's our job to start with ourselves and the people in our homes, and then spread the message of peace to our neighbors. This community event in New Wilmington encouraged all people of different races, religions, genders, and political views to gather in the name of "peace." It was a great example for our children to witness. Fred would have appreciated it.

Romans 14:19 (NIV) "Let us therefore make every effort to do what leads to peace and to mutual edification."

11.

I have also written a children's book entitled *PEACE IS.../PAZ ES* It's told through the eyes of Titan, my golden retriever. It's a collection of photos with Titan explaining what peace means to him. I was Titan's translator (dog Language is a gift of mine) and Debra Sanchez translated the English into Spanish. It's a simple book that hopefully will encourage families to "get the conversation started" about peace with their children. I think Fred would have enjoyed reading it and sharing it with his neighbors.

Be like Titan.

I can look into his eyes and see so much that is "unsaid" with unconditional love. I know it sounds impossible, but when Titan and I have our quiet moments (and there are many), I can see those who have gone before me in his eyes…it's almost as though they are saying, "I'm so happy that you have Titan."

Anyway, please consider publishing your own thoughts about peace.

12.

This past October, my Westminster students and colleagues were part of the town's Halloween Parade.

We dressed as crayons that represented the children's book, *Broken Crayons Still Color.* It is a story that provides children with tools to help them when "life happens." It is written by Toni Collier and, Whitney Bak, with illustrations by Natalie Vasilica.

Be like my college students and colleagues.

13.

Of course, Fred's key message that coincided with being a peaceful neighbor was being a KIND NEIGHBOR. In the year of 1997, Fred wrote a note to me. A portion of it read, "Most of my days now are used in writing scripts. I spent the first two weeks here working on the New Orleans speech. I'll send you a copy of that when I get a clean one (lots of last-minute changes) if you like."

Later, he sent a postcard from Florida that read, "Elaine Lynch (my asst.) will send you a copy of the NATPE speech.

(You could have been the one to have given the quote I paraphrased at the end!)"

On February 4th, I received my copy of his remarkable words from Elaine Lynch. The Mister Rogers' Institute has given me permission to share the quote that Fred used at the end of his speech.

He wrote:

"In closing, I paraphrase someone who lived and died long before the Advent of television: 'There are three ways to ultimate success: The first way is to be kind. The second way is to be kind. The third way is to be kind.' I wish you such ultimate success in all that you do."

It's an honor that Fred thought so kindly of me to think I could have been the author of the quote regarding "kindness." He knew how to make someone feel worthy.

Again, Be like Fred.

Chapter Thirteen
Closing Thoughts

How can we shine Fred's light? We can start in our homes with the knowledge of being mindful of what children hear and see on computers, phones, and televisions. I believe that children, below the age of two years, don't need any form of media or technology.

They need direct contact with loved ones in their families.

Stories need to be read.

Stories need to be told.

Curiosity needs to be modeled, encouraged, and applauded.

Creativity needs to be developed by providing experiences with the arts. And when creativity "happens," it needs to be showcased.

Introduce technology a little at a time and make sure you are with your child when they are using technology at the young ages.

There is no need for the young child (preschool to primary age) to be exposed to the news. As children grow into the preteen age, watch the news with your child. Talk about it. Make all conversations age-appropriate.

This is what Fred would do, so we need to carry the torch on behalf of him.

As an educator, I am very concerned with the representation of government on the federal level. During our friendship, Fred and I never spoke of our political beliefs. There was only one time Fred mentioned a politician in an 8/6/96 letter:

"I was in Washington for the Conference on Children's Television. All I can tell you is that the Clintons and the Gores seem to be very serious about their commitment to children. I think you'd really like them personally – no matter what your political ties." Clearly, Fred was able to find "good" in leaders without dwelling on their political affiliation.

I don't think "politics" was "polarized" to the point that it became a highlight in conversations between friends in the 1980s and 1990s. It never occurred to me to start a conversation with Fred about politics. Instead, we had many discussions about education and our faith.

One discussion centered around my teachers' union going on strike. After this discussion, Fred sent a card that had a photo of a man in a field holding a young lamb. He wrote:

"Dear Todd,

This card reminded me of you. Your heart holds so much. May this tough time of teacher "negotiations" end with unexpected healing. God can bring amazing good out of the darkest trouble. (witness Easter)"

I always shared my latest directorial work of First and Second Grade Musicals and my additional work with choral directing for the high school musicals with Fred. He always responded with such interest. He, too, would share his latest script writing and the complexity of the final product. This is just one of several instances he wrote about his preparation for a new series of shows:

"I'm trying to write some new scripts. As always, I'm grateful for your prayers."

You need to know that Fred spent countless hours writing his scripts. You may think that it was "easy writing" for him, but it was a complex task and he took it very seriously. He wanted every word to "count." He knew his words were helping to form the minds of children. He considered it an enormous responsibility.

Isn't it wonderful that Fred asked me to pray for him as he ministered to children while writing scripts for his show? What an honor to pray for a man who realized his significance as a contributor to helping children. Fred realized he couldn't write without the prayers of others. He was aware of the responsibility he held…the power in his writing.

In one letter, Fred shared his interview with Katie Couric on The Today Show. "Katie Couric and I have worked together before, and she really cares about children…just like you. We're a society of treasure carers, all of us."

As I stated, we really didn't talk about politics outside of its "educational realm." At the time of our friendship, I may have been naïve, but I believed both political parties had best intentions for the children of our country, so politics just wasn't a topic of conversation with us. I still believe this to be true, but we seem to be so vocal about other aspects that hide our united quest to help children.

Sometimes it is difficult to "remain on the sidelines." I am always disappointed when funding for an educational opportunity is denied by local or federal government, but what has really hurt my soul is the rhetoric being used by leaders in the public arena where children are listening. This has happened on both sides of the aisle.

As I have mentioned in an earlier chapter, I have devoted my entire life to children, so when my devotion is tarnished by hurtful words on the Public Stage for children to hear, I become deeply troubled. If only households could protect young minds from the words being shared on television, but my recommendation of shielding them from this rhetoric sometimes is ignored.

I think Fred would respond to how politicians have used inappropriate words to get their "messages across to our nation of listeners."

Words matter.

Name calling is not appropriate.

Hatred toward others is not appropriate.

We can do better.

In my opinion, Fred would be "sharing his concern" and people would listen. We have become a society where "anything goes." I expect leadership in our country to model the language we want our children to use. Are there moments when we mistakenly use unsuitable language? Yes, but today's world has allowed it to be common instead of rare. At the very least, we can make language appropriate when children are listening.

Furthermore, I question why we live in a society that always focuses on our quest to win, win, win. This isn't just a political issue, but more of a societal problem.

I wrote a children's book, *You Are a Masterpiece!* with illustrations by Shelly Bowden Dobi. The message of the book is to allow intrinsic rewards to be the instrument of what makes life successful. In other words, enjoy the journey that helped you achieve the "trophy." Always remember, you can't carry the trophy wherever you go, but you can take the memory of the hard work it took to earn the extrinsic reward in your heart.

The hard work becomes a part of who you are. The trophy is something that you dust around on a bookshelf. When we focus more on the journey, the disappointment when we fail is more of a learning experience.

Children need to experience failure and disappointment. We need to provide our children with the tools to assist them when failure happens. With the acknowledgement of failure and the teaching of growth through their losses, we are preparing our children for life.

Along those lines, I think we need to question if our "winning" is a "win for everyone."

When we win, do the starving children in Third World Countries win?

Do the children whose parents can't afford preschool win?

Do the children whose parents can't afford lunch money win?

Do we win when funding for Children's PBS Programming is cut?

Do we really win when others suffer?

I think Fred would ask these questions.

I ask these questions because our children can't, and yet children seem to be on the losing team for much of our winning. My concerns are not written in a form of attack.

Please know that my intention is to be an advocate for children through thoughtful questioning.

Fred spoke to Congress, asking for more federal funding, during the early stages of Mister Rogers' Neighborhood. He spoke calmly, directly, and peacefully. His presentation was, financially, extremely successful. Fred and I talked about his "negotiating" with Congress when I shared my thoughts about preparing for a Teacher Union Strike. It's important to state that financial cuts toward agencies that help children have been made on "both sides of the aisle" and has been going on for decades.

When all is said and done, is "winning" the only form of success that resonates with today's culture? I hope not, and I do have hope. I believe all of us can come together in the name of children to resolve many, if not all, of these problems.

I have hope.

In July of 2025, a church family of New Wilmington Presbyterian Church sang a song during the service. The family consisted of three generations. It gave me hope to see a family sharing their love for God with the congregation. The grandparents had passed down their love for church music to their children and then their children passed down the same love to their little ones. It was a moment that touched everyone in attendance. It represented HOPE for the future.

Thank you to The Forsberg Family. Fred would have been filled with hope for tomorrow.

Be like The Forsbergs.

I've also watched a three-generation family work together in our Community Garden on our church grounds. I witnessed the grandparents setting an example for their children and their grandchildren as each generation planted, watered, weeded, and harvested the crops, together. Thank you to the Romig and Hunter families. You are a shining example of HOPE.

Be like the Romig and Hunter families.

I marvel at another family's love for our community as they reach out through their God Given Gifts. The Mohr Family is also three generational. If you could see Jim and Jill Mohr's grandson, Johnny, weaving his way through different opportunities in our church, I think you'd see him and his grandparents and parents as shining examples of what is important in our world.

Be like The Mohr Family.

When I mention these three families at work to make our "neighborhood" a better place, I truly believe that Fred, if he were here, physically, would be reminding us (as he always did) to spend more time as a family. We are in need of a "family spirit" to wrap around our globe. Fred considered all of us his "television family." He would see the "family unit" as being a substantial solution to many of our society's problems.

As I mentioned earlier, we've found "neighbors" to be talking about how much we need Fred right now. I think that statement is very telling. When I hear that sentiment, I always reply by saying that Fred's message can be carried through us. We can be the vessel of his message. It's up to us. All of the wonderful contributors to society that I have mentioned in the past chapter are shining examples of what Fred would applaud. We just need to do it more often and intentionally.

Also, I believe that when we make mistakes, we should apologize. Whether it be on the Political Stage, Hollywood Stage, Church Stage, School Stage, or Neighborhood Stage, we can always apologize. I know I have made mistakes in the classroom, and I was always on "the apology train" when needed.

It's good to admit when you are wrong. It's not a sign of weakness. It's a sign of growth and being human. I pray the tide will turn and kindness will prevail. We can lead with dignity and character. Be the "neighbor" that Fred would want us to be.

As I mentioned in a prior chapter, we need to model silence like Fred did. Just take time to look at your surroundings. Listen to the environment. Write about it. Draw it. Share it. If we really think about it, so much of learning is free.

Praying is free.

Drawing is free.

Listening and Looking are free.

Smelling and Tasting are free.

Going for a walk is free.

Helping a neighbor is free.

Sometimes it's useful to be bored. When we are bored, we eventually find something to do that is much more meaningful than a cell phone. When we are bored, curiosity can take the lead and bring us to a place that is very thought-provoking.

Two friends of mine, Gregg Behr and Ryan Rydzewski have written a book, *When You Wonder, You're Learning: Mister Rogers' Enduring Lessons for Raising Creative, Curious, and Caring Kids*. (Hachette Book Group) They were guest speakers at Westminster College and conveyed the message in the book's title with such grace. They expressed their message as if Fred was standing right beside them.

I encourage you to read their book, with the Foreword written by Joanne Rogers, Fred's wife. I think it expresses everything an educator and parent wants to happen in their classroom and home to help build the tools their children need to become successful learners and "neighbors."

Be mindful. Fred was a Minister of Mindfulness before mindfulness was a "buzz word" for helping everyone with coping skills. I think Fred thought of "mindfulness" as being a part of life. Fred appreciated quiet times. Breathing. Exercising (he swam every morning). Praying. He was modeling mindfulness before it was in vogue. We need to carry that message of stepping away from the "business of life" and take time to be present with the "gift of life."

Fred, most always, ended every form of communication with me by stating the importance of my life. Here are a few closings to letters that seem worthy of sharing:

"How blessed your children are to have you (and obviously you feel that way about them too)! Giving children a happy beginning to their "formal" education is a gift which you have offered them for their whole life. Bravo again, Todd."

"Those students are so blessed to have you and your enthusiasm as part of their early lives. They will carry you with them all their days. Talk about influence…that's the very best kind."

"Young children are blessed to have you in their lives. Their whole attitude about learning is forever colored by their relationship with you…You are in my prayers. Thank you for your lovely letter.

Your friend,

Fred"

These words have made a Forever Imprint on my heart. His words give me the courage to help our families, homes, towns, states, and countries become a more civilized place to live and raise children. I had mentioned in the Foreword that my goal in writing this book was to help me put my friendship with Fred into perspective so that I could help share Fred's light. All I needed to do was open all his letters and take a trip down "Memory Lane."

All of Fred's words written for me were also written for you. I am convinced that if Fred had met you, he would have shared some of the same thoughts that would help you on your journey.

Please consider his words to me to be a connection to you. Let his words help you to be a beacon of light for our children.

Perhaps this is the time you will consider stepping outside your daily life of raising your own children or grandchildren to make a difference with children that are in the exterior of your immediate family. Fred and I would talk about how raising children is everyone's responsibility. We shouldn't turn away from problems that other children have in society.

Just because it's not your child, doesn't mean it's not your problem.

We should be part of the solution.

Maybe you will join a Preschool Board or School Board in your community to give back to organizations that helped you in raising your own children.

You could always start giving, financially, to organizations that support children with cancer or other diseases.

You could become a volunteer for Public Libraries that foster programs for children.

Joining your local Rotary may be something that you could consider, for this is an organization that reaches out to children near and far in many ways.

There are so many avenues that you can travel to make your journey more "child centered." The possibilities are endless.

So many of these possibilities will require "putting down the phone" and becoming communicators face to face. Technology is both a curse and a blessing. I believe that many of our answers to social growth can be more effectively addressed through personal interaction. If you reflect on all that I shared with you about Mike, Tracy, Jennifer, Stephanie, Mollie, Julie, Pete, Ellen, and Fred, you'll be able to recognize the "human connection" component to all of their successes. Very little technology was involved in all that they did to spread the Word of Kindness.

What would Fred want US to do? Let's try to move forward in peace. Be an instrument of the "good." It starts with each individual. Let's do it. Today, not tomorrow. Right now. Let this be your new beginning!

Peace,

Todd Cole, Teacher of Masterpieces

Afterword

It's important for every reader of my words to know that I realize that my friendship with Fred was only one of many that he formed and treasured with people across the country. Yes, we shared a unique love for ministering to young lives, and I think Fred wanted to celebrate that commonality, but he reached out to so many others to form friendships that were deep, genuine, and "Authentically Fred."

Earlier, I spoke of how Fred would end his letters with the word "Peace." Two other closing statements were, "Gratefully, Fred" and "Your friend, Fred." How grateful I feel to have known this man and how honored I am that he called me his friend. Even though you may not have personally known him, Fred was your friend, too.

Move forward and spread the light.

This book is finished, yet there is much more for me to share. Although this was a very important part of my life's journey, there are more words to be written when the time is right. For now, just know that I am grateful for your willingness to read about a friendship that helped me grow intellectually, spiritually, emotionally, and socially. May your life be blessed by anything or everything I have shared…icing on the cake.

P.S. For all who took the time to read my words, may I say, "Bye, bye, my dear."

Books I Recommend about Fred Rogers

So many of the words shared by these authors support what Fred shared with me. The book titles 1-6 are children's books and the rest of my list are for adults. Happy Reading!

1. *Fred's Big Feelings: The Life and Legacy of Mister Rogers* by Laura Renauld, illustrated by Brigette Barrager. Atheneum Books for Young Readers

2. *Hello, Neighbor! The Kind and Caring World of Mister Rogers* by Matthew Cordell. Neal Porter Books, Holiday House

3. *Mister Rogers' Gift of Music* by Donna Cangelosi, illustrated by Amanda Calatzis. Page Street Kids

4. *Mr. Rogers: Young Friend and Neighbor* by George E. Stanley, illustrated by Meryl Henderson. Aladdin Paperbacks

5. *The Story of Fred Rogers: A Biography Book for New Readers* by Susan B. Katz, illustrated by Can Tugrul. Rockridge Press

6. *Who Was Mister Rogers?* By Diana Bailey. Penguin Workship: An Imprint of Penguin Random House LLC, New York

7. *The World According to Mister Rogers: Important Things to Remember* by Fred Rogers. Hyperion Books

8. *The Simple Faith of Mister Rogers: Spiritual Insights from the World's Most Beloved Neighbor* by Amy Hollingsworth. Integrity Publishers

9. *Mister Rogers' Neighborhood: Children, Television, and Fred Rogers* by Mark Collins and Margaret Mary Kimmel, Editors. University of Pittsburgh Press

10. *The Good Neighbor: The Life and Work of Fred Rogers* by Max King. Abrams Press

11. *I'm Proud of You: My Friendship with Fred Rogers* by Tim Madigan. Ubuntu Press, Los Angeles

12. *Peaceful Neighbor: Discovering the Countercultural Mister Rogers* by Michael G. Long. Westminster John Knox Press

13. *Revisiting Mister Rogers' Neighborhood: Essays on Lessons About Self and Community*, edited by Kathy Merlock Jackson and Steven M. Emmanuel. McFarland & Company, Inc., Publishers

14. *The Mister Rogers Effect: 7 Secrets to Bringing Out the Best in Yourself and others from America's Beloved Neighbor* by Dr. Anita Knight Kuhnley. Baker Books: a division of Baker Publishing Group

15. *Everything I Need to Know I Learned from Mister Rogers' Neighborhood: Wonderful Wisdom from Everyone's Favorite Neighbor* written by Melissa Wagner, illustrations by Max Dalton. Clarkson Potter/ Publishers

16. *Dear Mister Rogers, does it ever rain in your neighborhood? Letters to Mister Rogers* by Fred Rogers. Penguin Books

17. *Fred Rogers: The Last Interview and Other Conversations* with an introduction by David Bianculli. Melville House

18. *The Last Interview and Other Conversations,* lyrics by Fred Rogers, illustrations by Luke Flowers. Quirk Books

19. *Mister Rogers' Neighborhood: A Visual History* written by Melissa Wagner, Tim Lybargen, and Jenna McGuiggan, with Foreword by Tom Hanks. Clarkson Potter/Publishers

20. *When You Wonder, You're Learning: Mister Rogers' Enduring Lessons for Raising Creative, Curious, Caring Kids* by Gregg Behr and Ryan Rydzewski. Hachette Book Group

Acknowledgements

Thank you to Gregg Behr and Ryan Rydzewski for allowing me to use their book within my text.

Thank you to The Fred Rogers Institute for granting me the privilege of using quotes he wrote in his letters to me.

Thank you to *Fred's Big Feelings: The Life and Legacy of Mister Rogers* by Laura Renauld with illustrations by Barrager, Atheneum Books, for the privilege of sharing a paraphrasing of your words about Fred's one way to relieve anger.

Thank you to Robert Berks' family for allowing me to use a photo of me posing by the statue of Fred in Pittsburgh.

Thank you to David Newell for allowing me to share one of his letters that he wrote to me.

ABOUT THE AUTHOR

Todd Cole is a teacher of children of all ages. Cole was a first-grade teacher for 25 years and a fourth grader teacher for 9 years. He considers Laurel Elementary to be a Holy Place…a place where teachers gather to help one another teach children, not the curriculum. Upon retirement, he embarked on a new venture of teaching students to become teachers at his alma mater, Westminster College. He has been a professor for The School of Education for 8 years. He considers this to be his continuation of "teaching children."

Todd enjoys spreading his love for children's literature by being a monthly guest on WFMJ TODAY in Youngstown Ohio. This is his 25th year with Channel 21. He writes quarterly editorials about All Things Education for local newspapers. You can often find Todd as a guest reader at libraries, preschools, and special events throughout the Western Pennsylvania area.

His work as a Rotarian of The New Wilmington Rotary Club is something he holds dear to his heart. It's a non-profit organization that helps people Here, There, and Everywhere.

He urges you to look into this organization in your own community.

Cole has written two children's books, *You Are a Masterpiece!* with illustrations by Shelly Dobi and *Peace Is.../Paz Es* written together with his dog, Titan. Todd has also written two "Teacher Advice" books...*50 Shades of Teaching* and *50 More Shades of Teaching/50 Sombras (más) de Enseñanza.* Two of these books were translated by Debra Sanchez, who also translated the Spanish portion of this book.

Cole is an active member of his church as an Elder, Worship Team, Chancel Choir, and Preschool Board. His church involvement helps him to "keep breathing." It is a source that assists him to express God's love for All people.

Todd is an active Alum for Westminster College having served as president of the Alumni Council and radio guest for Titan Radio. Westminster College is the physical space that helped him to form lifelong friendships that can be considered his "chosen family."

Todd shares his home with his golden retriever, Titan (named after Westminster College's mascot). Titan was at Todd's feet as he wrote this book. He is his constant companion and can bring a smile to the faces of New Wilmington when they travel around town in a convertible to catch a welcomed breeze on a sunny day.

Todd and Titan

Todd y Titan

Lenny and Hedda -
Two people Todd met on the set of The Land of Make Believe

Lenny y Hedda:
dos personas que Todd conoció en el set de grabación de The Land of Make Believe.

Above: Todd and Fred on the set of The Land of Make Believe.
Arriba: Todd y Fred en el set de grabación de The Land of Make Believe.

David Newell, aka Mr. McFeely, and Todd at a special event at WQED.

David Newell, alias Mr. McFeely, y Todd en un evento especial en WQED.

Left: Todd at the Fred Rogers Star on Pittsburgh's "Walk of Fame". Fred was among the ten original honorees in October of 2025.

Izquierda: Todd en la estrella de Fred Rogers en el «Paseo de la Fama» de Pittsburgh. Fred fue uno de los diez homenajeados originales en octubre de 2025.

Center: Todd at the Fred Rogers Memorial Statue ("Tribute to Children") on the North Shore in Pittsburgh.

Centro: Todd en la estatua conmemorativa de Fred Rogers («Homenaje a los niños») en la costa norte de Pittsburgh.

Right: Drawing of Fred by an exchange student from Costa Rica. She presented it to me on the last day of the semester in my Educational Psychology class.

Derecha: Dibujo de Fred realizado por una estudiante de intercambio de Costa Rica. Me lo regaló el último día del semestre en mi clase de Psicología Educativa.

A few of the letters from Fred that were mentioned in the book
Algunas de las cartas de Fred que se mencionan en el libro.

The Crooked House, Nantucket
Fred's summer home.
La casa de Verano de Fred

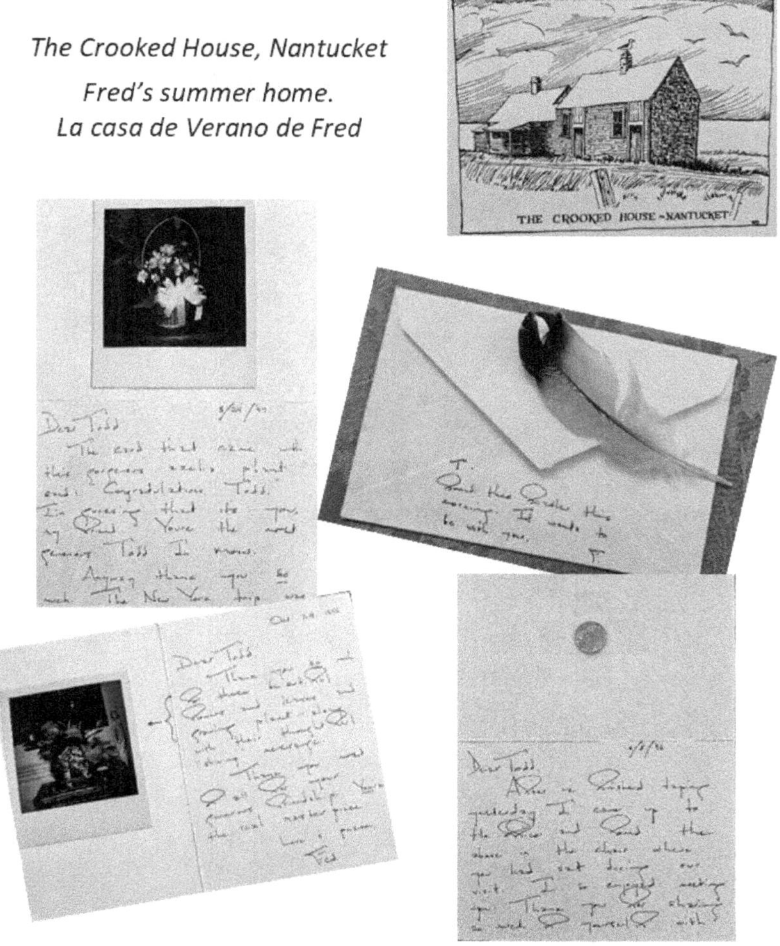

Fred and Todd came from strong families of love and faith.

Fred y Todd provenían de familias fuertes, llenas de amor y fe.

Above: Todd with his brother and parents.
Arriba: Todd con su hermano y sus padres.

Below: Todd's father and mother.
Abajo: El padre y la madre de Todd.

Below: Todd with his mother.
Abajo: Todd con su madre

The cover of this book.
La portada de este libro.

Fred and Todd loved the sunrise on the Atlantic. This is Todd's favorite photo from Well's Beach in 2024.

Fred y Todd admiraron el amanecer sobre el Atlántico. Esta es el foto favorita de Todd en Wells Beach en 2024.

Left: Beach time is special to Todd and his family.
Center: Todd's mother, brother, and nephew.
Right: Todd and Titan take morning and evening walks on Wells Beach.

Izquierda: La playa es un lugar especial para Todd y su familia.
Centro: Todd's mother, brother, and nephew.
Derecha: Todd y Titan dan paseos matutinos y vespertinos por Wells Beach.

Friends are family, too.
Todd with Ellen and Todd with his best friend Pete.

Los amigos también son familia.
Todd con Ellen y Todd con su major amigo Pete.

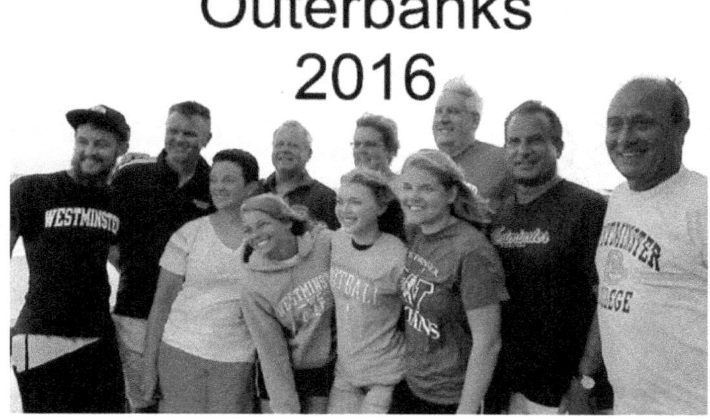

Todd's College Family Families
and "kids" who call him Uncle Todd.

La familia universitaria de Todd
y jovenes que lo llaman Tío Todd

Trolley Time!
¡Tiempo del tranvía!

TOPICAL FEATURED

Cole brings magic of Mr. Rogers to Laurel

Nancy Lowry
New Castle News 5 hrs ago 0

1 of 6

Todd Cole shares the wisdom of Mr. Rogers with first graders at Laurel Elementary School on Wednesday.

Nancy Lowry | NEWS Todd Cole shares the wisdom of Mr. Rogers with first graders at Laurel Elementary School on Wednesday.

More Trolley Time!
¡Más tiempo del tranvía!

Mike Case and I in my living room after our WFMJ-TV segment about Fred Rogers.

Mike Case y yo en mi sala de estar después de nuestro segmento de WFMJ-TV sobre Fred Rogers.

Fred always said, "I like you just the way you are!" and that each individual is special.
Fred siempre decía: «¡Me gustas tal y como eres!» y que cada persona es especial.

Below: Todd on the roof of Laurel Elementary school for "Reading All Day on the Roof".

Abajo: Todd en el tejado de la escuela primaria Laurel para «Leer todo el día en el tejado»

Below: Mike Case came to film a WFMJ-TV segment of the Reading All Day on the Roof event.

Abajo: Mike Case Vvno a grabar un segmento de WFMJ -TV sobre el evento «Leer todo el día en el tejado».

Literacy Under the Lights event at Wilmington Area School District.

Evento Alfabetización bajo las luces en el distrito escolar del área de Wilmington.

third-grade teacher in the Sharpsville Area School District, heard a presentation from Remake Learning – a Pittsburgh-area organization. Planning started in February.

NINA REIDER | New Castle News

Dr. Todd Cole acts out a book during Wednesday's Literacy Under the Lights event at Wilmington High School.

Event co-organizer Tracy Andrews, a first-grade teacher at Wilmington, said the event allowed them to fulfill their goal of sharing a love of reading and to get books into the hand of children.

"We have too many kids that don't have books at home," Andrews said.

Andrews said the initial plan was to have the event in the spring, but said it made more sense to have it near the beginning of the school year to coincide with football season.

The two worked with professors from Slippery Rock University and Westminster College, as well as regular and pre-service teachers and other community organizations to put on the event, which was

Through
guidance,
encouragement and
support young minds and
hearts flourish. In turn, those
young minds and hearts can nurture
a sapling into a majestic holiday tree,
like Trevor did.

A
través de
la orientación,
el aliento y el apoyo,
las mentes y los corazones
jóvenes florecen. A su vez, esas
mentes y corazones jóvenes pueden
nutrir un árbol joven hasta convertirlo
en un majestuoso árbol navideño,
como hizo Trevor.

The School of Education at Westminster College honored Fred's message of kindness.

La Facultad de Educación del Westminster College honró el mensaje de bondad de Fred.

Todd's examples impact young lives across schools and ages.

Los ejemplos de Todd influyen en las vidas de jóvenes de todas las edades y escuelas.

William Disman, Salutatorian of Laurel High School 2025 spoke of his time as a fourth grader in my class.

William Disman, segundo mejor estudiante de la promoción de 2025 de la escuela secundaria Laurel, habló de su etapa como estudiante de cuarto grado

Always REMEMBER to:

Be Kind like Fred

Recuerda siempre:

Sé amable como Fred.

Titan remembers.
Here he is dressed as Fred for Halloween.

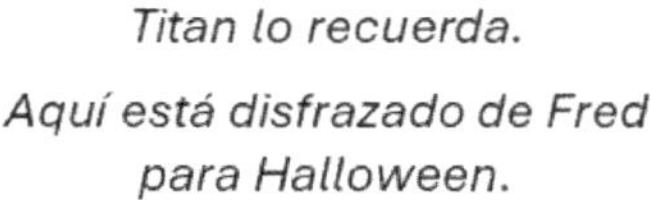

Titan lo recuerda.

Aquí está disfrazado de Fred para Halloween.

ÍNDICE

CAPÍTULO UNO

Nuestra amistad desde el principio

Es fundamental «preparar el terreno» para explicar cómo Fred llegó a ejercer una gran influencia en mi vida como educador y como ser humano. Conocer cómo evolucionó nuestra amistad le ayudará a comprender cómo he llegado a responder a la pregunta: «¿Qué haría Fred?». Así que, allá va.

Todo comenzó con un proyecto que mis estudiantes de primer grado enviaron a «Mister Rogers» en la década de 1980. Como mi distrito escolar formaba parte del mapa del oeste de Pensilvania, mis estudiantes ya conocían el programa Mister Rogers' Neighborhood de la cadena WQED de Pittsburgh. Era nuestra primera «publicación de un libro» del año escolar, «Nuestro libro de reglas escrito por las obras maestras del Museo 106».

Me refería a mis estudiantes como obras maestras y al salón de clases como un museo. Cada estudiante escribió una «regla» y dibujó una ilustración para explicarla. Luego, cada regla se copió y se convirtió en un libro utilizando mi encuadernadora, que unió cada regla con una espiral de plástico en el lado izquierdo del libro. Cada niño recibió su propia copia. Leímos el libro en voz alta varias veces antes de enviarlo a casa para que lo añadieran a su biblioteca doméstica de libros para leer con su familia. Enviamos una copia del libro al Mister Rogers y, como se suele decir, el resto es historia. (Por cierto, mis alumnos de primer grado escribían más de 20 libros por año y a menudo encontraba los libros expuestos en sus fiestas de graduación de la escuela secundaria. Nunca se sabe lo importante que pueden ser las palabras escritas por un niño en el tejido de su vida).

Mister Rogers (tenga en cuenta que aún no lo llamaba «Fred») respondió rápidamente con una carta en papel membretado de Mister Rogers' Neighborhood. Escribió sobre la importancia de las reglas en la vida para mantenernos a salvo. Compartió su agradecimiento por la forma en que cada estudiante sostenía el lápiz con tanto cuidado para dibujar imágenes que representaran cada regla. ¿Se imagina la emoción que sintió cada niño al saber que Mister Rogers apreciaba la forma en que sostenían el lápiz?

Para mí es muy importante reconocer cómo Mister Rogers llamó la atención sobre algo tan simple y, sin embargo, tan importante para un alumno de primer grado y su maestro. Debes saber que esto es lo que hace que los maestros, los teóricos, los ministros y Mister Rogers sean ESPECIALES para los niños pequeños. Las personas que trabajan en el «campo de ayudar a las mentes jóvenes a crecer» PIENSAN en lo que es importante para su público y luego lo reconocen de una manera adecuada para su edad. Mister Rogers era un experto en abordar lo que es esencial para la vida COTIDIANA de un niño pequeño. Sostener un lápiz correctamente era una de esas cosas.

No hace falta decir que hice una copia de la carta para cada niño y enmarcamos el original y lo colocamos encima de la estantería de la biblioteca del salón de clases.

A partir de ahí, Mister Rogers y yo nos convertimos en amigos por correspondencia y, en algún momento (con la ayuda de mi amiga Ellen), me llamó para invitarme a su «barrio» para grabar su programa de media hora. Me tomé un «día libre» y conduje hasta WQED en Pittsburgh, Pensilvania. Estaba a una hora y media de mi casa.

Recuerdo lo que llevaba puesto. Era una chaqueta azul y pantalones caqui con una corbata de SAVE THE CHILDREN. (Todavía los tengo). Estaba muy nerviosa. Nunca había conducido hasta Pittsburgh. Salí de casa muy temprano por miedo a perderme y llegar tarde... Les recuerdo que esto fue antes de los teléfonos móviles y Map Quest.

Llegué una hora antes, así que tuve tiempo de sobra para calmar mis nervios o acelerarlos (ustedes eligen). Cuando reuní el valor para entrar en el edificio, me dieron instrucciones de preguntar por Hedda. Ella acudió rápidamente en mi ayuda para recibirme con una sonrisa radiante y unos ojos que decían «bienvenido» incluso antes de decir una palabra. Me tendió la mano, que se encontró con la mía sudorosa, pero no pareció importarle. Mientras caminábamos hacia THE LAND OF MAKE BELIEVE (El País de la Fantasía), me contó que Fred estaba deseando conocerme «cara a cara».

Vaya. ¿Uno de mis héroes estaba deseando conocerme?

Por supuesto, yo estaba más que emocionado por conocer a un icono para los niños, pero el hecho de que él estuviera deseando conocerme me hizo sentir «especial». Esto, como todos sabemos, era uno de los mensajes dMister Rogers: todos somos especiales tal y como somos.

Mientras me acompañaba al estudio, allí estaba. El castillo se encontraba a la altura de mis ojos, a la izquierda del estudio, con el árbol en el centro y el reloj a su derecha. A la derecha había un piano de cola y, a lo largo de la pared, había carretes que mostraban los títeres que Mister Rogers utilizaba en varios segmentos del programa. The Land of Make Believe era brillante y hermoso. Espero haber «pintado el cuadro» con precisión. A medida que envejezco, me doy cuenta de que algunas partes de mi memoria están «afectadas».

Estaban ensayando un segmento con X el Búho. Me quedé a varios metros del árbol. Había varias sillas dispuestas que parecían ser para los invitados, así que supuse que una de ellas sería para mí. Mister Rogers estaba arrodillado detrás del árbol con el títere «X el Búho».

De repente, Mister Rogers me miró. Se levantó y salió de detrás del árbol. Fred, vestido completamente de negro, el color de la ropa para los títeres, estaba de repente frente a mí. Extendió su mano, que pronto se convirtió en un soporte para mis dos manos.

Luego, se echó hacia atrás, me miró directamente a los ojos y dijo: «Vaya, qué placer conocerte». A continuación, anunció:

«Atención todos, este es el maestro Todd, maestro de Obras Maestras y amigo mío».

Realmente no recuerdo lo que pasó después, pero al final me encontré escondido detrás del árbol con Mister Rogers, sosteniendo su guion mientras leía la parte de X el Búho. Me temblaba la mano mientras sostenía las páginas grapadas del diálogo, pero Mister Rogers nunca llamó la atención sobre mi nerviosismo. Estaba, literalmente, hombro con hombro con él, de rodillas, ya que el árbol no era tan ancho. Teníamos que estar ocultos de la vista de la cámara.

Para ser sincero, me sentía un poco incómodo estando tan cerca de otra persona a la que no conocía demasiado bien... pero, en realidad, supongo que sí lo conocía. Era «el vecino de todos». Más tarde, descubriría que habría otro «momento incómodo» que acabaría «anhelando y esperando» cuando nos encontrábamos de vez en cuando, pero no quiero «adelantarme».

Cuando terminó esta parte de la grabación, Mister Rogers me acompañó hasta su piano y tocó una improvisación caprichosa que indicaba a su equipo que la grabación había terminado hasta la tarde. Me quedé impresionado con su habilidad para tocar el piano. Le salía de forma muy natural. Yo también utilizaba el piano en mi salón de clases de primer grado como una forma de «transición» de un evento a otro. Tuve la suerte de tener en mi salón de clases un piano extra del departamento de música de nuestra escuela primaria. A menudo tocaba una melodía en el piano y les decía a mis estudiantes que, una vez que dejara de tocar, debían coger sus libros de lectura, que estaban en sus pupitres, y abrir la primera página de una historia determinada.

Volviendo a mi visita a WQED... Estaba mirando todo lo que formaba parte de la «magia» del Land of Make Believe , cuando Mister Rogers terminó su obra maestra y me sonrió diciendo: «La música es una parte muy importante de mi vida». Él sabía que me encantaba la música, porque le había escrito sobre cómo cantaba en el coro de la iglesia. Después de tocar su obra maestra en el piano, logré contarle cómo tocaba el piano en mi salón de clases. Me pidió que se lo explicara con más detalle, así que lo intenté.

Cuando digo «logré» e «intenté», hay que entender que estaba hablando con un héroe al que admiraba, y era un poco abrumador. Su genuino deseo de saber más sobre mí parecía hacer que las conversaciones posteriores fueran más relajadas.

Me acompañó hasta sus títeres mientras colocaba a X el Búho en su sitio asignado (un carrete). Compartió algunas de ellas conmigo. Se convertía en el personaje cada vez que colocaba un títere en su mano. Era fascinante. Mis ojos se abrieron como platos y mi corazón se llenó al darme cuenta de que estaba en presencia de un líder para los niños (y sus padres). Su amor por los títeres era evidente al mirar cada uno de los títeres que colocaba en su mano. Cada títere tenía un tono de voz diferente, pero la sonrisa en el rostro dMister Rogers al convertirse en cada personaje era la misma... sus ojos y sus expresiones faciales iluminaban la habitación. Estaba en su «elemento». Vi una alegría absoluta en su rostro.

También me quedó claro que se sentía orgulloso de lo que había creado cuando compartió algunos de los títeres conmigo.

¡Qué momento tan especial!

Olvidé mencionar que me presentaron a otros títeres, manejados por otros titiriteros, cuando tuve el honor de sentarme en el suelo (con las piernas cruzadas) detrás del castillo durante otra parte de la grabación. Uno de los hombres amables, en particular, era Lenny. Él «interpretaba» al Prince Tuesday (Príncipe Martes). Nunca volví a verlo, pero me causó una impresión positiva por ser un alma amable y gentil. Mister Rogers habló de él con amabilidad en algunas de nuestras correspondencias posteriores. Mister Rogers habló de la participación de Lenny en musicales, ya que Fred sabía de mi trabajo como director coral en los musicales de la escuela secundaria de mi distrito. Espero que Lenny lea esto y se dé cuenta del impacto que tuvo en mí nuestro breve encuentro. También me encantaría volver a ver a Hedda. Era una persona muy amable.

En fin, tras el momento de asombro con los títeres, Mister Rogers me acompañó a su oficina. Era una oficina muy modesta... se podría decir que estaba abarrotada. Como maestro, tiendo a compartir el «gen del desorden». Me han dicho que es un signo de creatividad... así que aceptémoslo. Supongo que la mayoría de las pilas de Mister Rogers contenían cartas de admiradores que el maestro de la escritura de cartas, Mister Rogers, debía responder personalmente, así como guiones y música para futuros segmentos. A menudo me escribía sobre su «próximo proyecto».

Mientras estábamos en su oficina, hablamos. No fue una «charla trivial». Quería saberlo todo, desde mi filosofía educativa hasta mi vida personal. Gran parte de mi vida ya la había compartido a través de cartas. Fue una larga conversación que, con el tiempo, supe que duraría toda la vida. Pero fue en ese momento cuando «Mister Rogers» se convirtió en «Fred» para mí. A partir de entonces, se sucedieron reuniones, muchas llamadas telefónicas y cartas. Compartí con él mis relaciones con mis padres y mi mejor amigo. Me encontré compartiendo mis preocupaciones sobre mis estudiantes, a lo que él respondía con palabras reconfortantes y animosidad.

Seguí haciendo que mis estudiantes le escribieran cada año, y él respondía con sus auténticas palabras escritas, que proporcionarían un recuerdo significativo a cada uno de mis estudiantes durante muchos años. Pero sería mi amistad personal con Fred la que me ayudaría a poner en perspectiva los «acontecimientos de la vida» y me asistiría en cada «etapa» del viaje de mi vida.

*Después de nuestro primer encuentro en el plató de The Land of Make Believe y de una visita llena de gracia a su oficina, recibí una carta de Fred.

He aquí una parte de sus palabras:

«Querido Todd:

Después de terminar la grabación de ayer, subí a la oficina y encontré lo anterior en la silla en la que te habías sentado durante nuestra visita».

Fred había pegado una moneda de diez centavos en la parte superior de la carta. Había encontrado una moneda de diez centavos en el cojín del asiento. ¿No es eso lo que mejor resume la esencia de Fred? No podía dejar que algo tan pequeño como una moneda de diez centavos se quedara sin devolver a su dueño.

Eso es «lo que Fred haría».

Capítulo dos
Estar solo

Una vez compartí mi deseo de casarme y tener hijos en una carta a Fred. Sentía que tener una familia era lo «normal», lo «esperado». Como soltero, es extraño estar en eventos que se centran en la «familia». Pasé por una época en la que me sentía incómodo y aislado. Fred me escribió una vez: «Mencionas a una esposa e hijos y que deseas tenerlos. Solo quiero que sepas que conocemos a bastantes personas «solteras» que viven una vida muy plena y orientada a los demás. De hecho, mi profesora principal, la Dra. Margaret McFarland, era una de ellas. Su dedicación a sus estudiantes y a sus estudios sobre el desarrollo infantil (así como a sus sobrinas y a los hijos de estas) ocupaba todo su tiempo. Ella marcó una gran diferencia en la vida de muchas personas».

A continuación, compartió historias sobre maestras de su vida como estudiante de primaria que nunca se casaron y «decidieron desde el principio que no tendrían maridos ni hijos, sino que se dedicarían a su labor educativa».

Terminó esa parte de la carta diciendo: «De alguna manera sentí la necesidad de reflejar eso ante ti». Así que, para responder a la pregunta «¿Qué haría Fred?», me concedió la gracia que necesitaba para comprender que «estar solo» es diferente a «sentirse solo». Creo que estar solo ha resultado ser una de mis cualidades más entrañables. Es un lujo que la mayoría de la gente no puede permitirse. (Recuérdamelo la próxima vez que me sienta solo).

Bromas aparte, las palabras de Fred me dieron el valor para sentirme más cómoda conmigo mismo. Sabía que quería ser el mejor maestro posible. Fred me ayudó a comprender que cada persona tiene su propio camino. Mi decisión de seguir un camino menos transitado, sin tener hijos, fue lo que me convirtió en quien soy. Sabía que no podía separar el trabajo de mi vida de una vida personal que tendría que «compartir». Dicho esto, admiro a todos mis colegas que han sido capaces de equilibrar su pasión por la enseñanza con el amor por formar una familia. Me sorprende y agradezco su ejemplo. Simplemente sabía que para mí sería demasiado difícil. Muchos colegas y amigos me decían que mis estudiantes eran «mis hijos».

A mí también me gustaría pensar eso.

Por ejemplo, acabo de volver de cenar a un restaurante local donde, inesperadamente, me senté junto a un matrimonio. El marido era uno de mis alumnos de primer grado de años pasados. No había hablado con él en años, pero reconoció mi voz cuando hablaba con la camarera, así que entabló una amable conversación. Durante nuestra charla, me enteré de que era su cumpleaños y que su esposa acababa de aceptar un trabajo como maestra de educación especial. ¡Qué alegría ponerme al día con la vida de un antiguo estudiante! Me alegró la noche. Le pedí discretamente a la camarera que cargara sus cenas a mi cuenta. Mi gesto fue un pequeño detalle por alegrarme la vida y honrarme con la oportunidad de enseñarle cuando estaba en primer grado.

Pronto descubrirás que mis estudiantes, compañeros de trabajo, mis propios padres y hermano, vecinos y amigos para toda la vida de la universidad se convertirían en lo que yo llamo «familia». Fred era y es parte de esa familia.

Así que estar solo se ha convertido en un motivo de consuelo para mí. Por supuesto, Titan, mi golden retriever, está tumbado a mi lado mientras escribo estos pensamientos... así que no estoy completamente solo. Además, tengo mi música. Me encanta escuchar a mi cantante favorita, Sandi Patty, mientras trabajo y conduzco mi coche.

Quizás algún día eso de estar solo cambie, pero por ahora este es mi lugar feliz.

Capítulo tres

Pérdida

Durante una conversación con Fred en su oficina, recuerdo que un hombre entró para hablar con él. Reconocí su voz como muy familiar, pero estaba de espaldas a mí y vestía «ropa de calle». Fred tuvo que presentarnos. Era David Newell, también conocido como el Sr. McFeeley. Me levanté de la silla y le estreché la mano. Para mi vergüenza, no la solté. Seguí estrechándole la mano. Al final, la solté sin que él me lo pidiera. Todos nos reímos porque no lo reconocí sin su atuendo de repartidor rápido. David y yo «reconectamos» muchos años después. Lo leerás en un próximo capítulo.

Después de que David se marchara, pronto me di cuenta de que Fred se estaba convirtiendo en parte amigo y parte consejero. ¿Por qué? Bueno, en un momento dado se hizo el silencio en la sala. El silencio es siempre una estrategia clave para los consejeros. Era como si Fred estuviera esperando a que yo guiara la conversación. Fue entonces cuando le conté mi preocupación por uno de mis estudiantes que vivía en una pequeña caravana con su madre.

Katlyn, mi alumna, era inteligente y guapa. No conocía a su padre, ya que él no estaba «en el panorama». Esto ocurría con frecuencia en mi salón de clases. Al principio del año recibía la lista de estudiantes con varios nombres que figuraban con madre, pero sin padre. A menudo, estos estudiantes eran asignados a mi salón de clases a petición de sus madres. Era un honor ser una «figura paterna» para estos estudiantes. Como maestro de primer grado, siempre sentí la responsabilidad de ser un modelo a seguir para los niños que no tenían un padre viviendo en sus hogares. Como muchos de ustedes saben, los maestros desempeñan muchas funciones... y la de «padre o madre» es una de ellas.

Esta era una estudiante muy especial. Katlyn vivía al otro lado de la calle de su abuela, que estaba muy involucrada en su vida. Una mañana, la mamá de mi pequeña estudiante de primer grado no se despertó. Había fallecido mientras dormía. Compartí este trágico suceso con Fred. Hablamos de la necesidad de estar «presentes en su vida».

Enseñar los sonidos del alfabeto y el reconocimiento de los números parecía tan insignificante en momentos como este. Fred y yo hablamos de la conexión que establecemos como educadores con nuestros estudiantes y que hace posible el aprendizaje. Fred, durante sus programas de televisión, tenía una forma de establecer una conexión personal con sus oyentes. Era muy hábil para llegar a cada niño a nivel personal mientras miraba a la cámara. A veces, esta conexión permite impartir lecciones que están «fuera del libro de texto del currículo».

Es importante señalar que los maestros de primaria pasan más horas despiertas con los estudiantes que los padres durante la jornada escolar. La hora de acostarse para los niños de primaria es (con suerte) entre las 8 y las 9 de la noche, lo que deja el periodo más largo de horas de vigilia en la escuela con sus maestros. Los maestros se convierten realmente en un «segundo padre o madre» para muchos. A mí, como atestiguarán muchos maestros, me han llamado «mamá», «papá», «abuela» o «abuelo».

Es un cumplido.

La transición de Katlyn sin su madre fue una etapa difícil en su vida. Me gusta pensar que la ayudé a superar algunas de las dudas y miedos que tenía al comienzo de su proceso de duelo. Fred me escribió después de nuestra conversación sobre la pérdida.

Me escribió: «¡Qué afortunados son (Katlyn y su familia) de tenerte en sus vidas en este momento!».

Es solo otro recordatorio de que gran parte de lo que un maestro tiene en su caja de herramientas proviene de la conexión personal que se desarrolla entre el maestro y el estudiante... Yo lo llamo «El libro de texto de la vida».

En la misma carta, Fred me contó la muerte de su director musical, Johnny Costa. «Como puedes imaginar, lo echamos mucho de menos. El próximo jueves comienza la grabación en el estudio. Será la primera vez en 30 años que tenga que entrar en el estudio sin que él esté «físicamente» allí». Le envié flores a Fred y él, fiel a su estilo, les hizo una foto con una Polaroid y me la envió en una carta de agradecimiento. Las cámaras Polaroid eran «cosa del pasado», pero no para Fred. (Aunque parece que están volviendo a ponerse de moda). No fue la única vez que recibí una foto Polaroid suya. La cámara Polaroid era su «inseparable».

Ahora que lo pienso, Fred era un hombre muy ocupado. No tenía tiempo para ir a Foto Mat (la pequeña «cabaña» de revelado de fotos que se encontraba en el centro del aparcamiento del centro comercial). ¿Me estoy haciendo viejo? En cualquier caso, las cámaras Polaroid permitían a Fred tener fotos instantáneas que podía enviar a gente como yo.

Otra pérdida que sufrió nuestra escuela fue la de un querido estudiante mío que murió de meningitis. Se llamaba Robby. Fue algo repentino. No fue como un diagnóstico de cáncer, en el que se tiene «tiempo» para aceptar el tratamiento previsto. Fue muy difícil de asimilar. Me enteré de su muerte a través de la «cadena telefónica» que utilizaba el profesorado cuando había un día de nieve. No podía creerlo. Me encontré pidiéndole a mi colega por teléfono que repitiera la noticia de la tragedia. Simplemente no me parecía posible.

Tuve a Robby en primer grado, pero murió cuando estaba en quinto. Robby tenía muchas ganas de vivir. Yo estaba desconsolado, como todos los que lo conocían. Yo tenía una amiga especial, Ellen (véase la página de dedicatoria), que se puso en contacto con Fred para contarle lo que había pasado.

Fred llamó en cuanto se enteró. Las palabras de consuelo brotaron del teléfono. Aunque no había visto a Robby a diario desde que dejó el primer grado, siguió dejándome un adorno navideño cuando estaba en segundo, tercero, cuarto y quinto grado. Su madre continuó con la tradición, después de su muerte, hasta lo que habría sido el último año de Robby. Tuve el honor de pronunciar el panegírico en el funeral de Robby. Aunque me mantuve fuerte durante el discurso, rompí a llorar en el último banco de la iglesia después de que terminara el servicio.

Me recompuse y volví a la escuela para dar clase el resto del día en primer grado. Eso es lo que hacen los maestros. Eso es lo que haría Fred. Mis estudiantes me necesitaban tanto como yo a ellos en ese día tan difícil de mi vida.

¿Soy solo yo, o el primer grado es un año único y muy especial para los estudiantes y sus familias? Creo que es un año mágico. La mayoría de los estudiantes entran en primer grado como lectores principiantes y salen como lectores fluidos, ¡listos para cualquier cosa! El crecimiento en nueve meses es inconmensurable.

Me pregunto si eso era lo que Robby y sus padres apreciaban de mí. Ser el maestro que le enseñó a leer y escribir, a sumar y restar, fue un honor increíble. Ser el maestro al que le pidieron que pronunciara el elogio fúnebre de su hijo fue un recuerdo inolvidable. Estoy llorando mientras comparto estas palabras con ustedes.

Así que Fred compartió conmigo el proceso de duelo, aunque no conocía a Katlyn ni a Robby. Utilizó palabras cuidadosamente elegidas para expresar su pésame. No se limitó a enviar una tarjeta de condolencia. Llamó por teléfono. Escribió una carta. Fue muy significativo. Fue un modelo a seguir para mí a la hora de ayudar a otros en situaciones trágicas.

Eso es lo que hizo Fred.

Es importante que comprendan que mi experiencia como docente (mi vida) se ha visto afectada por muchas otras dificultades, pero solo he decidido destacar algunas de las pérdidas. Hemos perdido a maestros y yo he colaborado en sus funerales con canciones, y siempre me conmoverán sus contribuciones a nuestros hijos. Los maestros ayudan a moldear la pasión de los demás, por lo que cuando perdemos a un compañero, perdemos una parte de nuestro «ser». Estos momentos cruciales en la vida de un educador son agotadores, pero nos recuerdan la importancia de quiénes somos.

Recuerdo que nuestro director compartió un «momento de silencio» por el intercomunicador durante los anuncios matutinos tras la muerte de una maestra. Las lágrimas corrían por mi rostro delante de mis alumnos de primer grado. Es en estos momentos cuando los niños se convierten en cuidadores. Mis estudiantes corrieron hacia mí para darme un «abrazo grupal», sabiendo que eso me reconfortaría. Creo que los niños son muy resilientes. Pueden reconfortar a los adultos. Las «compuertas» se abren cuando reflexiono sobre este recuerdo.

¿Sabéis que ese mismo día, durante el recreo, apareció un arcoíris sobre nuestra escuela? Lo que lo hizo tan significativo es que era un día sin lluvia. Toda nuestra escuela sintió que era «la obra maestra de Debbie», que nos hacía saber que estaba a salvo, curada y feliz.

Fue un regalo de Dios. El vínculo entre los maestros de mi escuela era muy fuerte.

Cuando perdemos a un maestro, perdemos a un miembro de la familia.

Una última reflexión sobre la pérdida (por ahora) y cómo podemos aprender a formar parte de la ayuda en la transición de nuestros días terrenales al cielo. Hubo un tiempo en que los miembros de mi coro de la Iglesia Presbiteriana de New Wilmington se turnaban para cuidar a una querida miembro de nuestro coro que estaba muriendo en un hospital local. Era una mujer soltera de unos setenta y cinco años. Tenía muy poca familia, por lo que los miembros del coro eran su familia. Hacíamos «turnos» de ocho horas para sentarnos con ella, cantarle y rezar con ella. Aunque podía hablar, era difícil entender lo que intentaba comunicar y, a medida que pasaban los días, se fue quedando en silencio, con la respiración entrecortada. Escribíamos en un diario que estaba a los pies de su cama, para que el siguiente miembro del coro estuviera «al tanto» de lo que había sucedido durante el turno anterior. Le escribí a Fred sobre esto. Su respuesta fue:

«¡Qué persona tan maravillosa eres! Muchas gracias por compartir algo tan personal conmigo. Me siento privilegiado por saber tanto sobre ti como tú confías en mí. Tu «vecina» tiene la suerte de contar con tu ayuda en esa importante transición... como nacer... a una nueva vida. ¡Qué consuelo estar con alguien tan cerca del cielo! Ese es el regalo que ella te hace ahora mismo».

Como he tenido el honor de estar con mi padre y con mi madre cuando exhalaron sus últimos alientos, las palabras de Fred me parecieron más ciertas que nunca. Mis padres me enseñaron mucho durante el último capítulo de su vida. Gracias, Fred. La pérdida es parte de la vida. Nos ayuda a moldear quiénes somos. Es un privilegio «proveer» a nuestros seres queridos mientras hacen la transición al lugar definitivo de paz.

Capítulo cuatro
Nuestras amistades

Con el paso del tiempo, sentí que nuestro vínculo seguía creciendo. En una carta a Fred, le conté mi amistad con mi compañero de universidad, Pete. Pete y yo éramos y seguimos siendo muy buenos amigos. Éramos hermanos de fraternidad. Yo fui su padrino de boda. Él y su esposa, Marj, me permitieron ser una parte importante de la vida de su hija desde su nacimiento hasta el último acontecimiento, su boda.

Sarah, su hija, me pidió que leyera las escrituras en su boda, que tuvo lugar en la Institución Chautauqua, en Chautauqua, Nueva York. (Por cierto, la librería de la institución tiene una maravillosa exposición de libros y recuerdos de Mister Rogers... La exposición de Fred Rogers se encuentra entre grandes figuras políticas como Ruth Bader Ginsburg y artistas como Van Gogh y Bob Ross).

Al intentar compartir mis relaciones con personas como Pete, creo que es importante explicar cómo un teórico de la educación en particular me ha ayudado a comprender la importancia de las amistades profundas. Eric Erikson, un teórico educativo que tanto Fred como yo apreciábamos, era conocido por desarrollar las ocho etapas del desarrollo psicosocial. Es en la sexta etapa, de los 20 a los 45 años, cuando Erikson sugiere que los seres humanos suelen encontrar a su «pareja de vida». Cuando enseño la teoría de Erikson en mi clase de psicología educativa, no dudo en informar a mis estudiantes universitarios de que nunca he encontrado a mi «pareja de vida», pero todas las demás etapas se cumplieron con tal entusiasmo que pude ser feliz y tener éxito en la vida sin completar esta etapa como deseaba Erikson.

Pete fue una de esas personas que me permitió formar parte de la crianza de su hija, ayudándome así a cumplir parte de la teoría de Erikson. Pete y Marj me permitían visitarlos una vez al mes los fines de semana. Me convertí en la «niñera» de Sarah durante todo el fin de semana. Pasaba la mayor parte del tiempo con Sarah, jugando al «restaurante» o a la «tienda». Veíamos Mary Poppins cada vez que los visitaba. Contábamos chistes sin sentido que nos hacían reír hasta llorar. Incluso le cambiaba los pañales (no con mucho éxito, pero lo hacía). Aunque no era un pariente consanguíneo, me asignaron el nombre de «Tío Todd» el primer día que sostuve a Sarah en mis brazos.

Comparto esto porque creo que es importante saber que, cuando tu vida no «encaja» en un molde habitual (como mencioné anteriormente en un capítulo sobre estar solo), debe haber seres queridos cerca que te inviten a formar parte de sus vidas para que puedas crecer y aprender a través de una «etapa» como la de Erikson.

Fred apreció mis pensamientos. Le inspiraron a escribir sobre una amistad suya:

«Tú y Pete debéis compartir una amistad muy especial. Es bueno que puedas tener amigos tan devotos. Mi amigo Jim era uno de mis amigos más cercanos desde que empezamos la escuela secundaria. (Fui su padrino de boda. Mi padre era como un padre para él, ya que lo acogió después de que su padre falleciera cuando éramos adolescentes). Fui al hospital todas las noches durante una semana después del trabajo (¡eran los días de la televisión en directo!) cuando el hijo de Jim, Bob, tuvo un accidente de coche. Al final de la semana, Bob falleció. Lo visité en Carolina del Sur (donde trabajaba para Westinghouse) justo una semana antes de que falleciera. ¡Llevaba varios años luchando contra el cáncer y cada día se fortalecía más en su fe! ¡Qué privilegio haberlo conocido! Las amistades como esa son un regalo de Dios. Escribirte esto ha sido una «buena terapia» (como tú lo llamas) para mí.

Tengo algunos amigos especiales de la universidad que me abrieron sus corazones y sus familias. Los Ryan, los Allston y los Frambe tienen hijos que me llaman «Tío Todd». He podido ser invitado a todos sus eventos especiales, desde graduaciones hasta bodas.

Es un honor ser una parte importante de sus vidas. Me maravilla el increíble «trabajo de crianza» que presencio en los hogares de mi familia inmediata y mis amigos. ¡Bravo!

También debo mencionar a mi hermano «real», John, que me invita a formar parte de la vida de sus hijos cada vez que nos reunimos. Vive en el hermoso estado de Vermont. Mi hermano ha adoptado a su nieto. Aunque es algo fuera de lo común, es más habitual de lo que se imagina. Hacia el final de mi carrera, parecía haber al menos una familia de abuelos como núcleo de la unidad parental de un niño. Mi hermano

John está haciendo un trabajo extraordinario. Fred estaría muy orgulloso de él. Sé que Fred sería el primero en aplaudir el buen trabajo de John y reconocería que hay todo tipo de familias que hacen que nuestro mundo sea especial .

¡Viva mi amable y gentil hermano! John, eres una obra maestra.

Espero con ilusión la próxima boda, el próximo bebé y las próximas vacaciones con estas personas tan especiales.

Gracias por ser como son.

Capítulo cinco

El don del silencio

A Fred le encantaba el silencio. Es una de las cosas que aprendí a amar de él. El silencio puede resultar incómodo para algunas personas cuando hay una «pausa» en la conversación. Este no era el caso de Fred. Cuando se quedaba callado, solo nos estaba dando tiempo para pensar. En una carta, mencioné cómo el silencio me daba momentos u horas para ser creativo.

Él respondió en una carta: «Obviamente, TÚ, Todd, reconoces el gran valor del silencio. ¡Hablaste de conducir y pensar, de tomarte tiempo para pensar! Me pregunto cómo podemos ayudar a los niños a descubrir esa parte importante de su vida. ¿Cómo podemos ayudarles a comprender que nutrir sus almas a través del silencio es algo muy importante... ¡muy profundo!?!».

Sus palabras me recordaron que el «tiempo de espera» después de hacer una pregunta era esencial. Debemos permitir que se produzca el proceso de pensar. Sus palabras dieron un nuevo significado a la frase «el silencio es oro».

Eso es lo que hizo Fred. Me ayudó a apreciar más el silencio.

Cuando estamos en silencio, escuchamos. Fred era un gran oyente. Escuchaba a las personas. Escuchaba a la naturaleza. He enseñado a mis estudiantes a escuchar haciéndoles dar un «paseo para escuchar» conmigo.

Caminábamos con nuestras tablillas y lápices en mano, anotando los distintos sonidos que oíamos en los salones de clases, los pasillos, las oficinas y el patio. Tengo pensado hacer lo mismo con mis estudiantes universitarios este otoño.

Hay muchos libros infantiles maravillosos sobre la habilidad de «escuchar». Cuando enseñamos los cinco sentidos en ciencias, un paseo para escuchar puede convertirse en un paseo por la naturaleza si nos tomamos el tiempo de salir del salón de clases y adentrarnos en el «mundo real».

Recuerden que los paseos para escuchar no requieren hablar. Para esta actividad nos basamos en nuestros oídos. Es estupendo volver a reunirse en el salón de clases para compartir los diferentes sonidos que cada persona ha oído durante el paseo. Después de nuestra discusión, mis estudiantes escriben y/o dibujan algo que han oído en nuestro paseo para escuchar.

Fred utilizaba mucho el silencio en sus programas. Si se toma el tiempo de reflexionar sobre su uso del silencio en cada programa, creo que se sorprenderá de cuántos segundos de silencio entre el delicado piano y el diálogo se incorporan en los episodios de The Neighborhood. Fred me contó que lo hacía deliberadamente, para que los niños tuvieran tiempo de procesar sus pensamientos... tiempo para pensar.

Recientemente, me pidieron que hiciera un breve vídeo para compartirlo con mi última clase de alumnos de cuarto grado, que se graduaran de la escuela secundaria en 2025. Me sentí honrado de que me recordaran. (Pensé que, como hacía ocho años que no daba clase en el distrito, se habrían olvidado del viejo Sr. Cole). Cuando vi el vídeo que había hecho antes de enviárselo a la clase de último curso, me di cuenta de que hacía pausas entre los pensamientos del vídeo. Debía de ser algo que, de forma intencionada o no, había aprendido de Fred y que había incorporado como parte de mi forma de transmitir información reflexiva a los estudiantes. El silencio puede ser muy poderoso, ya que nos da tiempo para reflexionar y dar sentido a nuestros sentimientos. Espero que mis graduados percibieran la conexión que intentaba establecer con ellos. Como mi «última clase», eran muy especiales para mí.

Asistí a su ceremonia de graduación en la escuela secundaria de Laurel, como lo he hecho con todas mis clases anteriores, y me sorprendió ser el centro de atención del discurso de William, que fue el segundo mejor estudiante de la promoción de 2025. A veces, no te das cuenta de la diferencia que marcas en la vida de los niños. Sus palabras me hicieron llorar.

Fred creía en expresar los sentimientos, de una manera apropiada. Llorar es una forma de expresar amor, tristeza e incluso alegría. En mi opinión, él fue el primero y el mejor en enseñar a nuestros hijos cómo lidiar con los sentimientos.

Sentirse enojado o triste son emociones muy profundas y complejas que los niños necesitan aprender a manejar. Fred era un experto en ayudar a los niños a lidiar con sus sentimientos.

Un verdadero don.

Capítulo seis

El océano

Compartíamos nuestro aprecio por el océano. Una vez, Fred me envió una pluma de un pájaro que encontró mientras paseaba por la playa en Florida. Metió la pluma en un sobre y en el reverso escribió: «T. encontró esta pluma esta mañana. Quiere estar contigo. F.».

¿Qué haría Fred? Fred era un ejemplo de aprecio por la naturaleza y compartía «regalos sencillos, pero muy importantes» con las personas que quería. La pluma es uno de mis regalos más preciados. Él, como siempre hacía, me enseñó el amor por la naturaleza y por escribir cartas como forma de comunicación profunda.

Fred también me escribía desde su casa de verano en Nantucket. Tenía papel de carta con un dibujo de la cabaña en el anverso, con la inscripción «The Crooked House-Nantucket» (La casa torcida de Nantucket). Al parecer, realmente era «torcida». Si buscas imágenes de Fred en

Google, encontrarás varias fotos de él paseando por la playa y contemplando las olas en silencio.

Trabajé en el negocio de mis padres durante 19 veranos en Wells Beach, Maine. Era una casa de campo y un motel familiar. Antes de comprar el negocio, nuestra familia había pasado las vacaciones en York Beach, Maine, todos los veranos cuando yo era niño. Saltar y zambullirme en las frías olas del Atlántico son algunos de mis recuerdos más preciados de la infancia. (El agua del océano de Maine era bastante fría, pero eso era parte de la sacudida inicial que aprendí a apreciar).

Sigo pasando las vacaciones en Maine cada mes de junio con mi golden retriever. Es mi lugar para rejuvenecer y simplemente pasear por la playa con mi perro, Titan. Visito todos los lugares favoritos de mi familia para comer. Asisto a la iglesia de mis padres y rezo desde la última fila. Me encanta especialmente ver el amanecer. Es un pedazo de cielo. ¿Cómo no apreciar este regalo de la naturaleza?

Aquí hay una «P.D.» de una de las cartas que Fred me envió:

«¿No es maravilloso tener "memoria"? ¡Podemos pensar en la costa incluso cuando no estamos allí! F.».

En algún momento de nuestra comunicación escrita, debí enviarle a Fred una postal con una bonita imagen del océano. Así comenzaba su siguiente carta:

«Querido Todd:

Muchas gracias por la preciosa postal. (¡Ya sabes lo mucho que me gustan las olas!)».

Otra correspondencia de una postal:

«Estaremos en Nantucket hasta el 9 de julio y luego volveremos a Pittsburgh. Aquí es PRECIOSO. Nadamos todas las tardes frente a la casa».

Fred era nadador. Nadaba todas las mañanas en una piscina cubierta en Pittsburgh. Rezaba mientras nadaba. Me lo contó durante una de nuestras conversaciones. Esta forma de ejercicio le ayudaba a mantenerse delgado, con 143 libras (65 kilos)... muy disciplinado. Tengo ese número (143) en la puerta de mi oficina en Westminster, porque representa las letras de «Te quiero».

La portada de este libro expresa nuestro deseo de contemplar la majestuosidad del amanecer sobre el océano. Expresa esperanza. Las olas son infinitas, al igual que nuestro afecto por hacer de la vida un lugar mejor para nuestros hijos.

Capítulo siete

Los acosadores

Fred y yo compartíamos nuestro amor por nuestros maestros, especialmente por los de primaria. Fueron fundamentales para guiarnos hacia nuestra vocación. Nuestros padres, como primeros maestros, fueron la base de todo. Sin embargo, nuestros maestros y padres no siempre veían lo que ocurría fuera de casa o del salón de clases.

Los acosadores eran otro vínculo común que compartíamos. Ambos fuimos acosados cuando éramos niños. Ninguno de los dos se lo contamos al otro. Leí sobre los incidentes que sufrió Fred de niño y su capacidad para superarlos. De joven tenía sobrepeso y sus compañeros le perseguían desde la escuela hasta su casa. Laura Renauld, autora del libro infantil *Fred's Big Feelings: The Life and Legacy of Mister Rogers (Los grandes sentimientos de Fred: la vida y el legado de Mister Rogers)*, con ilustraciones de Brigette Barrager y publicado por Athenaeum Books, compartió este episodio en el texto.

Aunque los obstáculos de nuestra infancia eran «temas tabú», creo que lo «tácito» fue un hilo que tejió una conexión profunda entre nosotros. Cuando reflexiono sobre mi infancia, creo que mi amabilidad se confundía con debilidad. Yo era muy gentil e ingenua, y quizá Fred también lo era. Creo que esas cualidades pueden resultar «incómodas» para algunos compañeros en la edad de la Escuela Media. ¿Quizás el acoso era la única forma que conocían de lidiar con ello?

Como adultos, Fred y yo no teníamos miedo de mostrar el lado «sensible» de nuestras personalidades. Como maestros de niños pequeños, nuestro trato era a menudo amable. Fred solía terminar las conversaciones telefónicas o los mensajes de voz con las palabras «Adiós, querido». Puedo decir con toda sinceridad que no recuerdo a nadie más que terminara una conversación con esas palabras. Sin embargo, yo utilizaba «querido» como una forma de afecto hacia mis estudiantes.

Creo que tendemos a dejar de usar esas palabras de afecto cuando nos hacemos adultos... especialmente los hombres. Las palabras de Fred eran sinceras y honestas. Él me consideraba «querido». Creo que es entrañable... un sinónimo de « estimado ». Por favor, no confundan la sensibilidad de Fred con ser femenino. Fred se sentía cómodo consigo mismo. Esto lo convertía en uno de los hombres más masculinos que conocía.

Ojalá más hombres fueran tan sensibles como Fred. Me pregunto cómo sería nuestro mundo si los hombres tuvieran menos miedo de mostrar sus sentimientos.

Eso es lo que hacía Fred.

Creo que Fred y yo teníamos una «constante». Era nuestra familia y nuestra fe. La familia y la fe nos ayudaron a lidiar con los insultos y las dificultades de los actos crueles. También creo que nos ayudó como adultos a formar nuestra misión de ayudar a los niños pequeños a apreciar quiénes eran y, con suerte, prevenir parte del acoso que sufrimos.

Para mí, el momento más difícil del acoso fue cuando mi familia se mudó a Connecticut a mitad del sexto grado. Dejaba un salón de clases autónomo en Nueva Jersey y me trasladaba a un programa departamentalizado en el que tenía varios maestros y un casillero con candado. Era algo muy extraño para mí. Aunque en mi anterior colegio me habían tomado el pelo, no tenía ni idea de lo que me esperaba como alumno de sexto grado, delgado, bajito y muy ingenuo. En la primavera de sexto grado, dos compañeros de clase que iban en el mismo autobús que yo escribieron las palabras «Maricón Vete a casa Vete lejos» con espuma de afeitar por toda la pared lateral de nuestra casa. Nunca olvidaré a mi padre abrazando a mi madre mientras ella lloraba al ver el mensaje que claramente iba dirigido a mí. En ese momento, pensé que «la palabra con m» significaba que yo llevaba «calcetines blancos».

Estaba muy protegido. Podría compartir muchas más historias embarazosas sobre mi «inocencia», pero eso daría para otro libro. Siguiendo adelante, sabía que esa palabra era un insulto. Mis padres intentaron hablar conmigo al respecto, pero yo no quería llamar la atención sobre ello. Las palabras habían sido borradas de la pared de nuestra casa, así que pensé que debía borrarlas de mi mente. Mi familia nunca me obligó a afrontarlo directamente. En cambio, nos sumergimos en la «vida familiar y religiosa» para curar las heridas.

Como adulto, miro atrás y me pregunto si lo habríamos manejado de otra manera si hubiera sucedido en el mundo actual, en el que hay libros infantiles sobre el acoso escolar y en el que hablar de ello en terapia está más «aceptado».

Hay una gran cantidad de programas y recursos contra el acoso escolar que no existían en la década de 1970. Les animo a que busquen este tipo de libro si se presenta una ocasión que puede ayudar a un niño a superar situaciones difíciles, como el acoso escolar.

Las situaciones más difíciles se produjeron cuando entré en la escuela secundaria. Recuerdo que, en mi primer año de escuela secundaria, un jugador de fútbol americano me metió la cabeza en mi casillero. En otra ocasión, me tiraron a las duchas, completamente vestido, después de la clase de gimnasia. Recuerdo que corría a casa después de la escuela, atravesando el bosque (un atajo), para llegar antes de que mi madre volviera del trabajo (era la secretaria de nuestra iglesia) y poder meter la ropa en la secadora. Quería «ocultar» lo sucedido a mi familia.

Con el tiempo, fui un poco más aceptado, al igual que Fred. Fred fue elegido presidente de su clase de último año. Yo fui elegido tesorero del gobierno de estudiantes y me votaron para ser acompañante en el baile de «Homecoming». Así que supongo que a alguien le caía bien, pero sin duda fue una época difícil para mí. Espero que aquellos que me acosaban hayan madurado y se hayan convertido en mejores personas.

Y, para ser sincero, yo también insultaba a otros. Creo que, como me acosaban tanto, elegí a una chica para burlarme de ella. Creo que estaba encaprichado de ella y burlarme era mi forma inapropiada de llamar su atención. Ojalá pudiera pedirle perdón. Intenté encontrarla en las redes sociales, pero no tuve suerte. Creo que las experiencias de la infancia pueden ser difíciles, pero si tenemos una «base familiar fiel y amorosa», eso puede marcar una gran diferencia.

Entonces, ¿Qué hizo Fred? ¿Qué hizo Todd? Creo que ambos decidimos utilizar nuestras experiencias de trato cruel y convertirlas en algo bueno para el futuro. Creo que Fred y yo utilizamos los acontecimientos de nuestro pasado para ayudar a crear un futuro más brillante para nuestros niños, centrándonos en cómo enseñarles a tratarse unos a otros.

Fred era el «rey de la amabilidad». Yo he intentado ser un ejemplo de amabilidad, sabiendo que a veces he fracasado estrepitosamente. Sin embargo, nunca perdí de vista la meta de ser lo mejor que podía ser para nuestros niños. En lo que respecta a Fred y a mí, creo que nuestras pruebas y tribulaciones como estudiantes nos convirtieron en los seres humanos que somos hoy en día, con ministerios separados, pero similares, en el ámbito de la educación. Los llamo ministerios porque sé que Fred llamaba a su programa «ministerio televisivo».

Como mencioné anteriormente, decidí dedicar mi vida a enseñar a los niños, por lo que también lo considero mi ministerio.

He compartido mis experiencias de «acoso escolar» durante mi infancia con todos los grupos de estudiantes universitarios. Mientras les contaba las historias, vi lágrimas, vi conmoción. Quería que supieran que me había convertido en un miembro exitoso de la sociedad, y esperaba que los «acosadores» también lo hubieran hecho.

Compartir mis experiencias desagradables arroja luz sobre POR QUÉ mi mensaje de «bondad» es tan crucial. Compartir mi trayectoria personal con compañeros desagradables nos une como seres humanos y hace que mi enseñanza sea más significativa. Enseña empatía. Permite que mis estudiantes universitarios sean «vistos y escuchados», ya que imagino que muchos de ellos han sufrido a manos y/o palabras de acosadores.

Hablando de empatía, ¿recuerdas cuando Fred hizo un segmento sobre «morir»? Hablé con Fred sobre ese segmento. Encontró un pez muerto en la pecera y lo enterró fuera de la Casa del Vecindario. Mientras enterraba el pez, compartió la pérdida de su perro cuando era niño y cómo le hizo sentir. En ese momento, los espectadores, jóvenes y mayores, se sintieron cercanos a un Fred. Estoy segura de que tuvieron experiencias similares y eso ayudó a crear un vínculo entre Fred y sus vecinos televisivos.

No solo enseñaba compasión, sino también empatía. Fred podía abordar temas difíciles a un nivel adecuado para los niños pequeños. Era un ejemplo para todos los adultos, de modo que esos temas no fueran tabú en sus hogares. Fred facilitaba a los padres la discusión de temas delicados.

Tengo una postal que Fred me envió desde Winter Park, Florida, con una foto del Rollins College (su alma máter). Le había enviado una carta sobre la muerte de uno de los perros de nuestra familia, Shadow.

Su respuesta fue: «Siempre recordaré cuando tuve que llevar a nuestra gata de 21 años al veterinario, que la ayudó a ir al cielo. Me quedé con ella hasta el final. Sabes que te tengo en mi corazón. Tú también eres una obra maestra».

Capítulo ocho

11 de septiembre

Todos recordamos el consejo de Fred durante su anuncio de servicio público después del 11 de septiembre. «Busquen a los que ayudan». Todo el mundo buscaba sabiduría, una forma de dar sentido a algo tan increíble. Fred se las arregló para mirar y escuchar a su alrededor a partir de las noticias del día, y vio y oyó a personas que se ayudaban unas a otras en momentos de necesidad. No pudimos cambiar lo que sucedió en nuestro mundo el 11 de septiembre, pero Fred nos ayudó a seguir adelante con el conocimiento de que las personas se ayudan unas a otras... algo muy divino.

Su familia le enseñó a «buscar a los que ayudan» y él nos transmitió este conocimiento.

Fue en ese horrible día en la escuela primaria Laurel cuando me pregunté por primera vez «¿Qué haría Fred?». En ese entonces, muy pocos maestros disponían de tecnología en sus teléfonos que les permitiera compartir lo que estaba sucediendo. Recibíamos «fragmentos de información» de la oficina del director por correo electrónico y una severa advertencia de que nos abstuviéramos de encender los televisores de nuestros salones de clases. Poco a poco, los maestros iban recibiendo mensajes de sus maridos, esposas y padres en los que reconocían los terribles acontecimientos. Primero un edificio, luego otro, luego el Pentágono y el campo en el condado de Somerset, Pensilvania. Recibí un mensaje telefónico de la madre de uno de mis estudiantes pidiéndome que le dijera a su hijo que estaba bien rezar.

No sabía cómo abordar las noticias nacionales con mis estudiantes de primer grado, ni siquiera si debía hacerlo, pero cuando pensé en Fred, lo tuve claro. Sabía que él querría que lo hiciera de forma adecuada para su edad. Así que, al final del día, pedí a todos mis estudiantes que se unieran a mí en un círculo. Fue entonces cuando les dije a mis estudiantes de la clase de obras maestras que hoy había ocurrido algo malo en nuestro mundo.

Les dije que sus padres les contarían lo sucedido cuando llegaran a casa, pero que lo único que necesitaban saber en ese momento era que ese círculo nunca se rompería y que yo siempre estaría allí para protegerlos. Creo que mis palabras estaban dirigidas tanto a mí como a mis estudiantes.

Los niños necesitan saber que el salón de clases es un refugio seguro para ellos. Si no se sienten seguros en su entorno, no se sentirán cómodos para aprender, para arriesgarse, para fracasar, para alcanzar metas, para llorar, para reír, para compartir, para amar.

Fred se alegró de cómo lo manejé cuando se lo conté en una conversación posterior. Le di las gracias por sus palabras, que siguen siendo válidas hoy en día. Cada vez que ocurre algo horrible en nuestro mundo, siempre hay un presentador de noticias que se refiere al consejo de Fred... Busca a los que ayudan.

Capítulo nueve

Una gran pérdida

El 1 de enero de 2003, vi a Fred en la televisión montado en un descapotable en el desfile The Rose Parade como Gran Mariscal. No sabía que Fred participaba hasta que lo vi en la televisión. Más tarde supe que Fred estaba muy enfermo. Tenía un tipo agresivo de cáncer de estómago. Fred murió menos de dos meses después, el 27 de febrero de 2003. Me uní al dolor de todos los estadounidenses.

En el gran esquema de las cosas, no era muy mayor. Tenía 74 años.

Yo estaba devastado. ¿Qué haría sin él? No más cartas. No más reuniones. Y lo que es más importante, ¿qué harían los niños sin él?

Tanto niños como adultos acudían a él en busca de orientación. Era nuestra «brújula llena de fe» a través de su ministerio televisivo y los significativos mensajes que compartía tras terminar las grabaciones de su «barrio».

Recibí una invitación para su funeral, que se celebró en Pittsburgh. Me enviaron dos entradas. Invité a mi amiga, Ellen, que compartió mi pérdida y fue fundamental para tocar mi vida a través de Fred. Mientras caminábamos unas cuantas manzanas desde nuestro aparcamiento hasta el auditorio, tuvimos que pasar junto a un grupo de manifestantes silenciosos. Yo no entendía el significado, pero Ellen sí. Ellen me agarró del brazo y me dijo que siguiera caminando.

Mi amiga me dijo que creía que se trataba de un grupo que viajaba por todo el país para protestar frente a los funerales de personas que luchaban por ideales contrarios a sus creencias. La explicación de Ellen era difícil de entender. Sabiendo que todo el mundo tiene derecho a protestar pacíficamente, me resultaba problemático. Estaba de duelo. ¿Cómo podía ser Fred, el «vecino» de todos, visto como algo más que un ejemplo de amor para la humanidad? Pero, de nuevo, era su derecho. Los pensamientos confusos cambiaron rápidamente, porque en el momento en que abrimos las puertas del vestíbulo del teatro, nos recibieron letras y dibujos de niños de todo el mundo que cubrían las paredes de arriba abajo.

Fue conmovedor.

Los pensamientos de los niños: «Gracias por enseñarme a ser amable». Estoy seguro de que a Fred le habría gustado que el vestíbulo se centrara en los mensajes de los niños. Después del servicio, tuve la oportunidad de dar las gracias a Joanne Rogers por compartir a Fred con todos nosotros. Solo la había visto unas pocas veces cuando asistí a los recitales de piano que ella y su amiga Jeannine dieron en el campus de mi alma máter, el Westminster College. También la vi en la fiesta de presentación de una biografía escrita por Max King que tuvo lugar en el Museo de Historia Infantil de Pittsburgh.

El funeral de Fred fue un servicio inspirador al que asistieron algunos de sus invitados favoritos del «vecindario», como Yo-Yo Ma. Estuvo lleno de música, que es lo que Fred hubiera querido. Fred era sin duda un músico talentoso. Escribió toda la música (letras y melodías) de cada producción de «Mister Rogers' Neighborhood». El funeral fue una forma de sanación para mí. Agradezco que Ellen, que ayudó a iniciar nuestra amistad, pudiera estar conmigo en el final de mi contacto terrenal con Fred.

Gracias, Ellen. Te estaré eternamente agradecida.

Después de la muerte de Fred, la vida siguió «sucediendo». Me encontré deseando que Fred siguiera vivo para apoyarme durante los acontecimientos que cambiaron mi vida.

Mis padres finalmente se mudaron para estar cerca de mí en New Wilmington, Pensilvania. Se unieron a mi iglesia. Disfrutaban de ser parte de mi vida como educador. Mi padre falleció después de que Fred alcanzara su Día de Gloria.

Después de la muerte de mi padre, me di cuenta de que Fred y mi padre trabajaban juntos como ángeles en una misión para ayudarme a continuar como educador de niños.

Estoy segura de que mi padre guiaba a mi madre mientras ella pasaba todos los días conmigo mientras me recuperaba del cáncer en un «hospital de larga estancia». Él le dio la fuerza para ser fuerte por mí... leyéndome oraciones y escrituras cuando yo podía oír, pero no podía concentrarme para leer debido a todos los medicamentos. Sé que tanto Fred como mi padre trabajaban como ángeles para ayudar a otros a ayudar a mi madre a mantenerse fuerte durante esos meses difíciles, llevándola en coche para que pudiera estar a mi lado todo el día, todos los días, en un hospital que estaba demasiado lejos para que ella pudiera desplazarse por su cuenta como mujer de 80 años. Aplaudo la fuerza y la fe de mi madre, que fue un ejemplo para todos cuando los visitantes venían a verme al hospital. Ella se mantuvo firme, pero estaba claro que contaba con un «sistema de apoyo superior».

Cuando me curé, me convertí en la cuidadora de mi madre, ya que ella padecía un tipo de cáncer terminal. Sé que mi padre y Fred (y otros miembros de la familia que nos habían «abandonado a medias») trabajaban a través de mi familia, amigos, colegas y miembros de la iglesia, ya que me apoyaban para que fuera fuerte por mi madre como su cuidador. Me encantaba leerle oraciones y cantarle al menos cuatro veces al día como un ritual que allanaba el camino hacia su Día de Gloria.

Durante la enfermedad de mi madre, estuvo confinada en una cama de hospital en nuestra terraza acristalada. Mi vecina hacía las compras para mi madre, para que yo tuviera algo que «abrir el día de Navidad». Hicieron una lista juntas, para que mamá pudiera participar en el proceso de intentar que las fiestas fueran especiales. El simple hecho de estar al lado de mi madre era el mejor regalo que podía haberme hecho, pero agradecía la alegría que le producía verme abrir los regalos que Maggie, nuestra vecina, había comprado en nombre de Mamá.

Pete, mi mejor amigo, al que mencioné en un capítulo anterior, nos visitaba todas las noches después del trabajo. Se sentaba junto a mi madre y a mí en las frías y oscuras noches de invierno en la terraza acristalada, mientras compartíamos buenos recuerdos. Esto era muy terapéutico para todos nosotros. Estoy seguro de que los miembros de mi iglesia y las personas de todo el país que formaban parte de las cadenas de oración estaban allí cuando mi hermano viajó innumerables veces desde Vermont. Sus oraciones mantuvieron a mi hermano a salvo mientras viajaba desde Nueva Inglaterra. Estaba claro que los ángeles y aquellos que viven entre nosotros me estaban ayudando a ser fuerte. ¡Qué regalo es para mí reflexionar sobre este tiempo sagrado y poder ver a Dios obrando a través de sus ángeles celestiales y terrenales!

Así que, aunque Fred no estaba «vivo» cuando murió mi padre, cuando yo pasé por el cáncer y cuando murió mi madre, él ESTABA allí... estaba trabajando «en concierto» con muchos otros. Creo que son aquellos que se han ido antes que nosotros los que nos guían en nuestro camino para convertirnos en mejores personas.

A veces converso con ellos para discutir un problema o para darles las gracias.

Capítulo diez

Reconectando

Después de la muerte de mi madre, me costó mucho renovar mi «propósito». Vivía con mi madre. Cuando le diagnosticaron un cáncer terminal, nuestro vínculo se hizo más fuerte que nunca. El hospicio venía una hora, dos o tres veces por semana, y yo tenía 14 horas a la semana de servicios externos para estar con mi madre mientras daba clases a los estudiantes universitarios. El resto del tiempo, Mamá y yo lo pasábamos hablando, viendo Hallmark y Jeopardy, rezando, cantando y durmiendo. Podía hacer mis tareas escolares mientras Mamá descansaba. Mi sillón reclinable (mi cama improvisada) se colocaba junto a la cama de hospital de mamá en nuestra terraza acristalada. A menudo, en la oscuridad de la noche, le cogía la mano y le daba tres golpecitos (uno por cada palabra de la frase «te quiero»). Ella siempre me devolvía los tres golpecitos.

Cuando murió, la casa quedó en un silencio sepulcral y ya no hubo más «golpecitos». Habíamos perdido a nuestro perro durante la lucha de mamá, por lo que el silencio de ser el único miembro vivo de la familia en la casa era ensordecedor.

Una persona, que observaba desde lejos, sabía que mi «primera Navidad» sin Mamá sería difícil. Se llamaba Jim Mohr. Era capellán del Westminster College. Su hija estaba a cargo del desfile anual de Navidad en un pueblo vecino. Jim se había puesto en contacto con uno de sus «vecinos» para que fuera el gran mariscal del desfile. Se llamaba David Newell, también conocido como Mr. McFeely.

Jim me preguntó si estaría dispuesto a recoger a David Newell en el hotel para llevarlo al recorrido del desfile. Por supuesto, respondí con un alegre «¡SÍ!». Jim ya había establecido una estrecha amistad con David, y sentí que Jim sabía que yo necesitaba levantar el ánimo.

¡Fue una gran sorpresa! Tuve la oportunidad de volver a conocer a David y compartir «historias de Fred» con él mientras lo llevaba al lugar del desfile. Pude regalarle un ejemplar de mi libro infantil *You Are a Masterpiece!*

Antes del desfile, había hecho carteles para que mis estudiantes universitarios, colegas y actuales hermanos de la fraternidad los sostuvieran mientras caminaban por Main Street. Mi amigo Pete organizó a los hermanos de la fraternidad para que llevaran los carteles.

Yo hice una pancarta, que llevaron mis estudiantes universitarios, en la que se leía: «¡Westminster College te agradece que seas su vecino!». Me quedé con David, que iba vestido con el traje completo de Mr. McFeely, durante toda la noche, mientras él estaba sentado en el frío junto al árbol de Navidad de la ciudad, firmando autógrafos a una fila de fans.

Cabe destacar que el árbol para el desfile de la ciudad del año anterior fue donado por la familia de uno de mis antiguos estudiantes. Era un árbol que le regalé a Trevor hace treinta años, cuando era un plantón, en el Día de la Tierra, en primer grado. Había crecido hasta alcanzar un tamaño enorme, , y tenía una forma perfecta y estaba adornado con luces de colores brillantes. No hace falta decir que mi corazón estaba lleno esa noche, y creo que Dios estaba trabajando muy duro por mí a través de Jim Mohr, David McFeely, la familia de Trevor, mis compañeros de la universidad, mis estudiantes, mis amigos y mi fraternidad.

¡Las estrellas se alinearon esa noche tan especial!

Mientras mi madre se aproximaba a su «muerte terrenal», me hizo prometer que compraría otro golden retriever cuando fuera el momento adecuado, porque sabía que me sentiría solo. Compartí esto en una carta con David (el Sr. McFeely) cuando tomé la decisión de abrir mi corazón a otro miembro de cuatro patas de la familia. Su respuesta:

«¡Un golden retriever! Debes gustarte los perros activos... ¡Tenemos un mastín inglés de 90 kilos y él, «Bear», es un adicto al sofá! ¡Es un perro encantador... come como un caballo!».

Le había pedido su opinión sobre un nombre para mi golden. Había reducido la lista a dos nombres, Titan (la mascota del Westminster College) o Dyson (como la aspiradora, debido a todo el pelo que suelta el golden retriever). La respuesta de David:

«Creo que me gusta Titan, ya que se relaciona con WC y la zona donde vives... ¡aunque Dyson es más divertido! Avísame cuando te decidas... Apuesto a que estás impaciente». (Estaba esperando la mágica separación de «ocho semanas» de mi cachorro de su madre). TITAN fue la opción elegida por la mayoría de mi familia y amigos, ¡así que TITAN fue el elegido!

En otra ocasión, tuve el honor de compartir un rato con David cuando habló en un servicio en la capilla de Westminster. ¡Vino en su 80.º cumpleaños! El reverendo Jim Mohr me pidió que encargara una tarta para celebrar su cumpleaños. Tuve el privilegio de llevarla a la capilla con velas encendidas y una multitud de «vecinos» cantando ¡FELIZ CUMPLEAÑOS!

Creo que Fred estaba/está contento de que hubiera vuelto a conectar con David. Él está mirando hacia abajo y sonriendo. A través de estos acontecimientos con David, Jim Mohr me ayudó a darme cuenta de que cada final es un nuevo comienzo. Mi conexión restablecida con David McFeely sigue viva y en buen estado. En un capítulo posterior verán cómo David/el Mr. McFeely ayudó a más personas de mi comunidad.

Volví a encontrarme con David en el Cardigan Day, en noviembre, cuando se celebró en WQED. Fue un evento que permitió que todos los que querían a Fred se reunieran en un mismo lugar... ¡qué regalo! Fui con mi amiga de Pittsburgh, Ellen, que sabía más que yo sobre cómo conducir en Pittsburgh. (Para ser sincero, casi todo el mundo sabe más que yo sobre cómo conducir en una ciudad). Conocí a un nuevo «vecino», Chris, que había viajado desde Connecticut solo para estar en presencia del espíritu de Fred. Esto es un verdadero testimonio de la gran influencia de Fred. Chris era/es director de una escuela cristiana en Connecticut.

Recuerdo que me quité el pin del tranvía que llevaba esa noche de mi cárdigan rojo y se lo di a Chris. Seguimos en contacto a través de mensajes de texto en días festivos y ocasiones especiales que nos recuerdan a Fred y al barrio.

¿No es agradable conocer a nuevos vecinos que comparten el amor por Fred? ¡Qué manera tan estupenda de unirnos en la esperanza por el mañana y en la misión de hacer del mañana un mundo mejor para nuestros hijos! Sin duda, fue una noche mágica llena de alegría.

Mi reencuentro con David nunca habría ocurrido si no fuera por el reverendo Jim Mohr. Es un hombre que trabaja como siervo de Dios.

Capítulo once

Fe

Ambos teníamos una fe muy fuerte, pero nunca mostramos nuestra religión en televisión ni en los salones de clases. Por «mostrar nuestra religión» me refiero a que no recitábamos las escrituras para los vecinos de la televisión ni para los estudiantes en los salones de clases. Creo que veíamos la fe de Fred cada vez que lo veíamos en Mister Rogers Neighborhood, y sin embargo él nunca mencionaba la religión en antena. Eran sus amables palabras, sus expresiones agradables y sus pensamientos cariñosos los que creaban una conexión con sus espectadores.

Como maestro, mi misión era establecer esa misma conexión con mis estudiantes, que pudiera crecer a lo largo del año para dar vida al currículo, recordando que no enseñamos el currículo, sino a los niños. Sin la conexión entre Fred y sus espectadores, y la mía con mis estudiantes, el mensaje podría perderse.

Así que, al igual que Fred, espero que mis estudiantes fueran testigos de mi fe al jugar con el estudiante solitario en el patio o al sentarme junto al estudiante de la clase que desprendía un hedor diario por su ropa sucia. Quizás vieron mi fe en el simple trazo de la tiza en la pizarra y en los coloridos carteles del tablón de anuncios. Quizás vieron mi fe cuando asistí a sus eventos deportivos y/o musicales fuera del horario escolar. Y tal vez, solo tal vez, vieron mi fe cuando utilicé mi día libre para «leer en el tejado de la escuela» durante todo el día... demostrando que se puede leer en cualquier lugar... incluso en el tejado de una escuela.

Creo que es innegable ver nuestra «fe en acción» en nuestro trabajo diario en la televisión y en los salones de clases. Creo que otra conexión que teníamos era que ambos éramos presbiterianos.

Al igual que Fred, es posible que ellos hayan visto mi fe en nuestra rutina diaria de escribir el horario en la pizarra y en la posición de mi cuerpo en la puerta cada mañana cuando entraban al salón de clases. Fred tenía una rutina... el mismo comienzo y final del programa, la misma alimentación de los peces. La rutina es una «red de seguridad» o «una manta favorita» que los estudiantes aprecian a cualquier edad. Ambos la modelamos.

Recientemente visité la iglesia de mis padres en Maine mientras estaba de vacaciones con Titan. La iglesia, pequeña en superficie, era grande en amor mutuo y por el Señor. El ministro concluyó con el mensaje de crear un «lugar seguro» para que todos se sintieran bienvenidos y amados. Compartió la importancia de ser un servidor y una persona de carácter, ya que el carácter proporciona esperanza.

Hablé con él después del servicio para agradecerle sus palabras y decirle que su forma de expresarse me recordaba a Fred (su cadencia y las pausas entre frases para permitirnos pensar y asimilar sus palabras).

Inmediatamente me dijo: «Gracias». Su respuesta fue tan rápida que me confirmó que sabía exactamente lo que yo quería decir. Sabía a qué me refería y lo consideró un verdadero cumplido.

Luego, procedió a contarme que había conocido al «oficial Clemmons». Mi respuesta fue que Fred se había adelantado a su tiempo en lo que respecta a acoger a personas de todos los colores en su vecindario.

¿Recuerdas cómo Fred compartió un pequeño piscina de agua para remojarse los pies junto al oficial Clemmons? Fred también secó los pies de Francois Clemmons (alias oficial Clemmons). El pastor Greg estuvo de acuerdo. Ojalá hubiéramos podido continuar la conversación. Quizás algún día lo hagamos. El motivo por el que menciono mi visita a esta iglesia es para recordarnos a todos que Fred realmente deseaba un mundo en el que las personas fueran aceptadas y amadas por lo que eran... proporcionando ese «lugar seguro» al que acudir. El pastor Greg compartía el mensaje de Fred, el mensaje de Dios.

Creo que es importante crear «lugares seguros» para TODOS los niños (de todas las razas, géneros, identidades sexuales y creencias religiosas) en las escuelas públicas. Este es un tema candente que ha causado muchos desafíos entre mis amigos de las redes sociales. Ha hecho que algunos cuestionen mi fe... discrepando con quién soy y en qué creo. A veces es doloroso, pero al igual que yo defiendo mis creencias, ellos también lo hacen. Se deben animar las opiniones diferentes, siempre y cuando no se expresen con el propósito de herir a los demás.

Cada generación ha tenido desafíos sociales, como los derechos civiles, el voto, el sida, el matrimonio entre personas del mismo sexo y los transgéneros, por nombrar algunos. Desgraciadamente, parece que todos los problemas sociales se han mezclado a gran velocidad durante la década de 2020.

Supongo que lo que intento decir es que nuestra fe es algo que se puede medir por cómo nos tratamos unos a otros. Nuestra fe se puede compartir con palabras amables. Cuando somos amables, creo que somos siervos fieles. Creo en la separación entre Iglesia y Estado.

Sin embargo, sí creo en el «momento de silencio». Esto permite a los estudiantes tomarse un tiempo para rezar o pensar en algo «feliz», lo que permite a todos los niños practicar su propia fe, y no la fe elegida por un distrito escolar.

Una vez más, el silencio es un momento que nos da el poder de pensar, rezar o simplemente crear un momento de atención plena.

¿Alguna vez has oído hablar de la oración del alfabeto? A veces, cuando no encontramos las palabras para expresar nuestros pensamientos en la oración, basta con cantar la canción del alfabeto. Cada letra del alfabeto está en cada palabra que buscas cuando no sabes cómo expresarlo.

Creo que deberíamos ser más expresivos cuando vemos a Dios obrando en nuestras vidas y señalárselo a los demás. Fred lo hacía todo el tiempo. Fred aplaudía la obra de Dios en nuestras vidas simplemente haciendo saber a sus vecinos de la televisión que le gustaban tal y como eran... compartía los pensamientos de Dios con los niños al otro lado de la pantalla.

Fred lo hacía sin necesidad de centrarse en el nombre de Dios en su programa, sino glorificándolo con sus pensamientos y acciones. Creo que cuando compartimos ese mensaje, compartimos la historia de Dios, no nuestra historia. Debemos ayudarnos unos a otros para hacer de nuestros barrios un lugar más amoroso en el que vivir. Debemos sacrificarnos por nuestros vecinos, y no debemos hacerlo para impresionar, sino para ser dignos. Mi pastor de la Iglesia Presbiteriana de New Wilmington siempre nos anima a salir de las paredes de nuestra iglesia para ayudar a nuestro vecindario. Gracias, pastor Matt. (Por cierto, a Matt también le gusta Fred).

Cada mañana, antes de poner los pies en el suelo junto a mi cama, digo en voz baja: «Padre, úsame». Es sencillo. Quiero que me utilicen para mejorar el mundo que me rodea. Espero que mi explicación sobre mi fe te haya ayudado a comprender cómo actúo en un mundo que a menudo parece estar «conectado a un respirador artificial».

¿Me canso? Por supuesto. Cuento con las personas que me rodean y con mi fe para apoyarme en los momentos difíciles.

Cabe destacar que doy clases en la tercera planta del Old Main, que es el edificio más alto del campus... el lugar más cercano al cielo en el Westminster College. Para mí, es un recordatorio de que «los maestros son un regalo del cielo» y de que en nuestra profesión nos guía el mejor maestro de todos.

Capítulo doce

¿Qué querría Fred que hiciéramos?

¿WWFWUTD? (What would Fred want US to do?)

Todo el mundo, incluido yo, ha dicho: «Nos vendría muy bien tener a Mister Rogers ahora mismo». Cada día es más difícil desenvolverse en el mundo. Tenemos una tarea que cumplir. Fred me dice que tengo que llevar su luz. Fred sería demasiado humilde para llamarla «su luz», sino más bien «la luz de Dios». Creo que es responsabilidad de todos nosotros llevar su visión, su mensaje.

Me gustaría organizar este capítulo asignando un número a cada evento de cómo hemos comenzado a compartir la luz de Fred.

1.

Cuando ocurrió la masacre de la escuela primaria Sandy Hook el 14 de diciembre de 2012, todos buscábamos respuestas en otras personas. Es NUESTRA responsabilidad hacer un cambio para mejor. Podemos hacerlo, de forma pacífica. Yo lo hice escribiendo un editorial sobre mi visita al

Memorial de Sandy Hook. Lo hice comunicando a mis seres queridos que, en lugar de regalos de Navidad, enviaría una donación en su nombre a Sandy Hook Promise, una organización sin ánimo de lucro que promueve la legislación para obtener más fondos para la salud mental y una reforma sensata de la legislación sobre armas.

Es difícil «mantener la cabeza a flote» cuando ocurren estos tiroteos. Cada vez que hay un tiroteo en una escuela, casi me paralizo. Pero entonces recuerdo: «¡Busca a los que ayudan!». Vi a muchos corriendo en ayuda de la escuela y los hospitales locales. También me encontré animando a mis amigos de Facebook a que hicieran donaciones a organizaciones sin ánimo de lucro como Sandy Hook Promise y a que compartieran libros infantiles que ayudan a los niños a superar las secuelas de los tiroteos en las escuelas.

Tenemos que ser parte de la solución.

2.

En mayo de 2025, fui entrevistada en la cadena de televisión por cable de nuestra universidad por Benjamin Kelly, estudiante de la carrera de Radiodifusión. Gran parte de nuestra «charla», que iba a centrarse en el próximo evento del Rotary, Peace in the Park, dio un giro para convertirnos en una conversación sobre Fred y nuestra conexión con la «paz». Benjamin señaló en nuestra entrevista que, en nuestra correspondencia por correo electrónico para preparar la entrevista, yo siempre terminaba mis mensajes con «Paz, Sr. Cole».

Me preguntó por qué lo hacía. Le conté a Benjamin que empecé a terminar todas las cartas a mis alumnos de cuarto grado, a los padres y a mis compañeros con la palabra «paz» después del tiroteo de Sandy Hook. Me cambió mucho. Nuestra conversación sobre la paz y Fred pareció ser significativa para Benjamin. Este fue el reflexivo correo electrónico que me envió después de nuestra entrevista:

«Espero que hayas disfrutado de tu participación en la mesa redonda de Titan Radio. Fue un placer conversar contigo. Rara vez una entrevista me deja tan impresionado como para recordarla dos semanas después. Sin embargo, tus palabras y tu ideología hacia los demás me conmovieron tanto que me he sentido casi más ligero en las semanas siguientes. Buscar a los que ayudan y lo mejor en los compañeros y profesionales.

Gracias por tu cortesía y amabilidad durante la entrevista. Me encantaría volver a conectar contigo pronto.

Paz,

Benjamin Kelly

Este es otro ejemplo de lo significativo que puede ser escribir una carta o un correo electrónico para expresar tus pensamientos. Benjamin, como estudiante universitario, fue más allá de la responsabilidad de un presentador de noticias del campus.

Sea como Fred y sé como Benjamin.

3.

Después de la muerte de mi madre, mis compañeros de Laurel Elementary y Westminster College, junto con los miembros de la iglesia, se reunieron en las escaleras de la capilla con luminarias que formaban la palabra «PAZ». Me emocionó mucho. Eso es lo que Fred querría que hiciéramos.

Querría que nos ayudáramos unos a otros en las dificultades de la vida.

Estad ahí para vuestros seres queridos. Dejad el móvil y conectad con ellos cara a cara. Lo que mi familia elegida hizo por mí esa noche requirió mucha preparación con el reverendo Mohr, mi profesorado de WC y Laurel, los amigos de mi madre y mis mejores amigos, como Pete y Marj. Habían trabajado todo el día y, estaban dispuestos a reunirse para apoyarme en una noche muy fría.

Sea como todos ellos.

4.

Después de la masacre de Tree of Life (Árbol de la Vida) en Pittsburgh, Fred ya había alcanzado su día de gloria, pero su esposa Joanne y Tom Hanks (que estaba en la ciudad para el rodaje de una película de Mister Rogers) compartieron palabras de consuelo en una manifestación por la paz tras el tiroteo en la sinagoga.

Joanne dijo: «Reemplacemos las armas por abrazos» (Facebook, KDKA-TV, Pittsburgh, 8 de noviembre de 2018). Creo que Fred habría compartido un mensaje similar. Su declaración abordaba tanto la reforma de las armas como la salud mental al mismo tiempo. Eso es lo que habría hecho Fred. Pedí a mis estudiantes de la clase de Psicología Educativa que crearan un Árbol de la Vida con sus nombres en las hojas del árbol para exhibirlo en nuestro salón de clases. Crear arte puede ser una forma de abordar el dolor o de permitirnos reconocer un acontecimiento de una manera significativa y personal.

Sea como Joanne... da abrazos.

5.

Otra vía que he recorrido para difundir la luz de Fred es compartir con mis estudiantes universitarios de la clase de Psicología Educativa un vídeo titulado «*Our Assignment from Fred Rogers*» (*Nuestra misión de Fred Rogers*), producido por estudiantes de escuela secundaria del distrito escolar de Fox Chapel. En él se recogen entrevistas a niños de preescolar, al personal de Fred y a actores de televisión, a Joanne, a sus hijos y a Max King, autor de la biografía «*The Good Neighbor: The Life and Work of Fred Rogers*» (*El buen vecino: la vida y obra de Fred Rogers*). En resumen, esto proporcionó una hermosa visión de cómo Fred creó un lugar especial para que los niños pequeños, junto con sus familias, experimentaran formas de superar los momentos difíciles y celebrar los momentos de alegría. Abrió la puerta al cariñoso personal de Fred y a cómo veían el trabajo de Fred en «tiempo real». Este documental, que se puede encontrar en YouTube, tuvo una gran influencia durante el último semestre. Tuve una estudiante de intercambio de Costa Rica que vino a visitarme durante un semestre y que nunca había oído hablar de Mister Rogers. Fue a través de mis historias y de este vídeo/documental que esta estudiante desarrolló un verdadero amor por el ministerio televisivo de Fred.

El último día de clase, mi estudiante me regaló un dibujo que había hecho de Fred y Daniel el Tigre. No hace falta decir que se me saltaron las lágrimas. Fue un gesto muy significativo y amable por parte de una joven a la que probablemente nunca volveré a ver. He enmarcado su dibujo y forma parte de mi «Museo de Mister Rogers» personal. Doy las gracias a Ryan Devlin, del distrito escolar de Fox Chapel, por permitirme compartir este documental con ustedes.

Sea como los estudiantes de Fox Chapel con Ryan Devlin como su asesor.

Sea como Estefanny, de Costa Rica. Esforzaos al máximo.

6.

Guardo un grato recuerdo de Mike Case, presentador de un programa matutino de televisión local, que emitió un reportaje desde mi casa muchos años después de la muerte de Fred. Nos sentamos en mi salón y «simplemente hablamos» de Fred. Le mostré cartas. Compartí momentos que he comentado con ustedes en este libro .

Cuando se emitió el reportaje, la copresentadora de Mike tenía los ojos llorosos. Sus emociones eran sinceras.

Todos guardamos un recuerdo muy especial de Fred y, a veces, nuestro amor por Mister Rogers nos hace sentir emociones intensas. Creo que mi conversación con Mike Case transportó a todos los espectadores a un lugar de su infancia que les inundó de recuerdos de una época más inocente. El mensaje de Fred era muy sencillo, pero profundo.

Sé amable.

La experiencia de Mike en el campo de la radiodifusión ayudó a crear una imagen para los espectadores, permitiéndoles tomarse un momento antes de comenzar su día para ser parte de algo especial. Mike les dio «permiso» para hacer una pausa en su ajetreada mañana y volver a su infancia. Mike Case y yo seguimos siendo buenos amigos, y le agradezco su talento para captar lo que Fred significaba para mí durante ese segmento. Esa fue la forma que tuvo Mike de compartir a Fred con nuestro vecindario. Mike ayudó a los espectadores adultos a conectar entre sí al reflexionar sobre su propio amor por Fred.

Me gusta pensar que el segmento ayudó a los espectadores a reflexionar sobre cómo podían celebrar la contribución única de cada uno a la sociedad, desafiándolos a ser parte de la solución siendo mejores vecinos unos para otros.

Sea como Mike.

7.

Tengo una compañera educadora que ahora enseña a alumnos de primer grado en el aula 106 de la escuela primaria Laurel... la misma aula en la que yo enseñé a alumnos de primer grado hace tantos años. Se llama Stephanie Hennon.

Ella ha respondido a la pregunta: «¿Qué querría Fred que hiciéramos?». Stephanie organizó una semana temática titulada «¿Quieres ser mi vecino?» en conjunción con el Día del Cardigan, el 13 de noviembre, y la próxima película protagonizada por Tom Hanks como Fred Rogers.

Me dijo que en marzo celebramos la Semana del Dr. Seuss, así que ¿por qué no celebrar la Semana de Mister Rogers en noviembre? Stephanie llegó incluso a llamar a la Autoridad de Tránsito de New Castle para preguntar si estarían dispuestos a enviar un tranvía a la escuela primaria Laurel para utilizarlo como lugar de lectura de cuentos, con ella como narradora.

Bueno, ¿quién no haría algo especial en honor a Fred? La Autoridad de Tránsito «¡cumplió!». Se podría decir que fue una «entrega especial». Proporcionó un «escenario» perfecto para mi narración sobre Mister Rogers.

Decoré el interior del tranvía con frases como «¡Bienvenidos al barrio!» y «¡Son especiales!». El tranvía fue un escenario único que proporcionó un recuerdo especial a los niños, ansiosos por aprender sobre su vecino de la televisión.

Stephanie pidió a todos los maestros que decoraran los tablones de anuncios de los pasillos en honor a Fred. ¡Vaya! ¡Deberíais haber visto la creatividad! ¡Eran increíbles! Stephanie estaba difundiendo la luz de Fred a otra generación. Demostró que él sigue con nosotros en espíritu y que su mensaje sigue vivo.

Gracias, Stephanie. ¡Eres una obra maestra!

Sea como Stephanie.

8.

¡Les presento a la Sra. Tracy Andrews y a la Dra. Jennifer Toney, que han dado a conocer la misión de Fred de una manera muy especial! Me presentaron el «frED Camp», un campamento anual que ofrece a los maestros nuevas técnicas y estrategias para desarrollar el espíritu crítico, la curiosidad y el amor por el aprendizaje. Todo el día tiene como tema subyacente el espíritu de Fred. REMAKE LEARNING (recrear el aprendizaje) el, una organización sin ánimo de lucro, es la patrocinadora del taller anual. Más de 200 maestros se reúnen un sábado por la mañana en mayo para aprender, compartir ideas y simplemente disfrutar de su amor común por Fred Rogers. Sin duda, es un día especial para todos los que asisten.

El año pasado, el taller se celebró en el Instituto Fred Rogers, en la ciudad natal de Fred, Latrobe, Pensilvania. Si alguna vez tienes la oportunidad de visitar este museo, te aseguro que merecerá la pena el viaje.

Tracy y Jennifer también encabezaron un evento anual en el campo de fútbol de nuestro distrito escolar llamado «¡Leer bajo las luces!». Tuve la oportunidad de leer *Mister Rogers' Gift of Music,* escrito por Donna Cangelosi con ilustraciones de Amanda Calatzis, a los niños que vinieron a celebrar la lectura bajo las luces del estadio de fútbol en una fresca noche de otoño. La autora escribe sobre cómo Fred tocaba (y a menudo golpeaba) el piano cuando quería aliviar sus emociones de ira. Así que, después de terminar de leer esta maravillosa historia a los niños, coloqué cinco teclados en el césped verde del campo de fútbol. Dejé que los niños «golpearan» las teclas para imitar y recordar cómo Mister Rogers lidiaba con sus sentimientos de ira, que finalmente se convertían en algo melódico y pacífico después de rendirse a pensamientos más felices.

Como mencioné anteriormente, la música era una parte esencial de la vida de Fred. La utilizaba como herramienta para ayudarle a lidiar con un abanico de emociones y se convirtió en una parte integral de sus segmentos televisivos Neighborhood. Si tienes la oportunidad de «revivir» sus programas, observarás cómo la música ocupaba un «lugar central» cuando presentaba a músicos invitados. Para mí, su uso de la música me pareció más significativo cuando sustituía al diálogo. Unas pocas notas de piano mientras Fred alimentaba a los peces podían ayudar a que la «tarea» pareciera caprichosa... divertida.

«Gracias» a Tracy y Jennifer por ser maestras en el campo de la educación. Estas dos maestras están haciendo lo que Fred querría que hicieran.

Sea como Tracy y Jennifer.

9.

Disfruto siendo voluntario/lector invitado en la preescolar de nuestra iglesia. Oh, cómo disfruto viendo cómo las mentes más jóvenes brillan a través de sus expresiones faciales mientras paso una página tras otra de un libro que les inspira a convertirse en lectores. Es un privilegio. Además, no puedo expresar la gratitud que siento hacia Mollie y Julie, que son la maestra y la asistente de nuestros niños de preescolar. Trabajan muy duro con paciencia y amor. No se les paga lo suficiente por la «vocación» que han abrazado con tanta disposición. Son las primeras «maestras oficiales» de los niños, tanto en lo académico como en lo social y lo emocional. Utilizo la palabra «oficiales» porque todos sabemos que cada padre o madre es el «primer maestro» de un niño.

Sea como Mollie y Julie, y considere ofrecerse como voluntario para leer a las mentes jóvenes.

10.

Tenía el deseo de crear una forma especial de mostrar la PAZ en nuestra comunidad. Muchas de las tarjetas de Navidad de Fred tenían un mensaje de PAZ. Una de las tarjetas tenía palomas blancas y la palabra PAZ escrita en seis idiomas diferentes... era una tarjeta patrocinada por UNICEF.

A menudo terminaba sus cartas a mí firmando «Gracia y paz, Fred» o «Shalom, Fred». Con mi misión de crear un evento por la paz, aproveché mi condición de miembro del Club Rotario de New Wilmington para poner en marcha el DÍA DE LA PAZ EN EL PARQUE. Gracias al reverendo Jim Mohr, compañero rotario, David Newell, alias Mr. McFeeley, visitó el DÍA DE LA PAZ EN EL PARQUE como nuestro invitado especial.

La cola de adultos con sus hijos para conocer a David era larga, pero mereció la pena la espera. Mientras hablaba con sus fans, que esperaban pacientemente, la conversación no giraba en torno a la necesidad de volver a casa o al campo de béisbol de la liga infantil. Se centraba en sus recuerdos de Fred. Esperar en la cola era un privilegio, ya que todos compartían historias sobre sus episodios favoritos y cómo la serie les había ayudado a lidiar con sus propios sentimientos. David dedicó tiempo a cada familia. Era sincero y auténtico, igual que Fred.

David es una obra maestra.

Sea como David.

Contamos con estudiantes universitarios de la Facultad de Educación del Westminster College, que proporcionaron manualidades con temas relacionados con la paz para que los niños las crearan. Contamos con autores locales de libros infantiles que hablaron con los niños y presentaron sus libros.

Tuvimos una hora del cuento para los más pequeños y patrocinamos clases de arte para los niños. La música corrió a cargo de los estudiantes de la Facultad de Radiodifusión y Titan Radio. Se ofreció a nuestros invitados un camión de comida con comida haitiana . Hicimos un desfile de banderas de todo el mundo mientras cantábamos «Let There Be Peace on Earth», compuesta por el equipo de compositores Sy Miller y Jill Jackson Miller.

Este año, nuestro Club Rotario plantó un POSTE DE LA PAZ DE ROTARY INTERNATIONAL en nuestro parque comunitario. En los cuatro lados del poste está escrito «Que la paz prevalezca en la Tierra» en ocho idiomas diferentes. Los líderes de nuestra ciudad compartieron citas, poemas, pensamientos y oraciones que explicaban lo que significaba para ellos la «paz».

Yo compartí una reflexión sobre la paz que Fred compartió una vez. Habló de cómo podemos seguir en guerra con nosotros mismos y entre nosotros, aunque no estemos en conflicto con otro país mediante la fuerza militar. En otras palabras, podemos estar en guerra en nuestros hogares, escuelas, comunidades, estados y países.

Es nuestro deber empezar por nosotros mismos y por las personas de nuestros hogares, y luego difundir el mensaje de paz a nuestros vecinos. Este evento comunitario en New Wilmington animó a todas las personas de diferentes razas, religiones, géneros y opiniones políticas a reunirse en nombre de la «paz». Fue un gran ejemplo para nuestros hijos. A Fred le habría gustado.

Romanos 14:19 (NVI) «Por lo tanto, esforcémonos por hacer lo que conduce a la paz y a la edificación mutua».

11.

También he escrito un libro infantil titulado *PEACE IS.../PAZ ES*. Está narrado a través de los ojos de Titan, mi golden retriever. Es una colección de fotos en las que Titan explica lo que significa la paz para él. Yo fui el traductor de

Titan (el lenguaje de los perros es un don que tengo), y Debra Sanchez tradujo el inglés al español. Es un libro sencillo que, con suerte, animará a las familias a «iniciar la conversación» sobre la paz con sus hijos. Creo que a Fred le habría gustado leerlo y compartirlo con sus vecinos.

Sea como Titan.

Puedo mirarle a los ojos y ver tantas cosas «no dichas» con amor incondicional. Sé que suena imposible, pero cuando Titan y yo tenemos nuestros momentos de tranquilidad (y hay muchos), puedo ver en sus ojos a aquellos que se han ido antes que yo... es casi como si dijeran: «Estoy tan feliz de que tengas a Titan».

En fin, por favor, considera publicar tus propios pensamientos sobre la paz.

12.

El pasado mes de octubre, mis estudiantes y colegas de Westminster participaron en el desfile de Halloween de la ciudad.

Nos disfrazamos de lápices de colores que representaban el libro infantil *Broken Crayons Still Color*. Es una historia que proporciona a los niños herramientas para ayudarles cuando «la vida da un giro». Está escrita por Toni Collier y Whitney Bak, con ilustraciones de Natalie Vasilica.

Sea como mis estudiantes y compañeros de la universidad.

13.

Por supuesto, el mensaje clave de Fred, que coincidía con ser un vecino pacífico, era ser un VECINO AMABLE. En el año 1997, Fred me escribió una nota. Una parte decía: «Ahora dedico la mayor parte de mi tiempo a escribir guiones. Las dos primeras semanas aquí las pasé trabajando en el discurso de Nueva Orleans « » (El camino hacia la paz). Si quieres, te enviaré una copia cuando tenga una versión definitiva (hay muchos cambios de última hora)».

Más tarde, me envió una postal desde Florida que decía: «Elaine Lynch (mi asistente) te enviará una copia del discurso de la NATPE. (¡Podrías haber sido tú quien diera la cita que parafraseé al final!)».

El 4 de febrero recibí mi copia de sus extraordinarias palabras de parte de Elaine Lynch. El Instituto Mister Rogers me ha dado permiso para compartir la cita que Fred utilizó al final de su discurso.

Él escribió:

«Para terminar, parafraseo a alguien que vivió y murió mucho antes de la llegada de la televisión: "Hay tres caminos para alcanzar el éxito definitivo: el primero es ser amable. El segundo es ser amable. El tercero es ser amable". Les deseo ese éxito definitivo en todo lo que hagan».

Es un honor que Fred pensara tan bien de mí como para creer que yo podría haber sido el autor de la cita sobre la «amabilidad». Él sabía cómo hacer que alguien se sintiera valioso.

Una vez más, sea como Fred.

Capítulo trece

Reflexiones finales

¿Cómo podemos hacer brillar la luz de Fred? Podemos empezar en nuestros hogares siendo conscientes de lo que los niños ven y oyen en los computadores, los teléfonos y los televisores. Creo que los niños menores de dos años no necesitan ningún tipo de medio de comunicación o tecnología.

Necesitan el contacto directo con sus seres queridos en sus familias. Hay que leerles cuentos.

Hay que contarles cuentos.

Hay que animar, aplaudir y dar ejemplo de curiosidad.

La creatividad debe desarrollarse proporcionando experiencias con las artes. Y cuando la creatividad «surge», debe mostrarse.

Introduzca la tecnología poco a poco y asegúrese de estar con su hijo cuando utilice la tecnología a edades tempranas.

No es necesario que los niños pequeños (de preescolar a primaria) estén expuestos a las noticias. A medida que los niños crecen y llegan a la edad preadolescente, vea las noticias con su hijo. Hable sobre ellas. Haga que todas las conversaciones sean apropiadas para su edad.

Esto es lo que haría Fred, así que debemos continuar con su legado en su nombre.

Como educador, me preocupa mucho la representación del gobierno a nivel federal. Durante nuestra amistad, Fred y yo nunca hablamos de nuestras creencias políticas. Solo hubo una vez en la que Fred mencionó a un político en una carta del 6 de agosto de 1996:

«Estuve en Washington para la Conferencia sobre Televisión Infantil. Lo único que puedo decirte es que los Clinton y los Gore parecen tomarse muy en serio su compromiso con los niños. Creo que te caerían muy bien personalmente, independientemente de tus afiliaciones políticas». Está claro que Fred era capaz de ver lo «bueno» de los líderes sin fijarse en su afiliación política.

No creo que la «política» estuviera «polarizada» hasta el punto de convertirse en un tema destacado en las conversaciones entre amigos en los años 80 y 90. Nunca se me ocurrió iniciar una conversación con Fred sobre política. En cambio, tuvimos muchas discusiones sobre la educación y nuestra fe.

Una de ellas se centró en la huelga de mi sindicato de maestros. Después de esta conversación, Fred me envió una tarjeta con la foto de un hombre en un campo sosteniendo un cordero. Escribió:

«Querido Todd:

Esta tarjeta me ha recordado a ti. Tu corazón es muy generoso. Que este difícil momento de «negociaciones» con los maestros termine con una curación inesperada. Dios puede sacar un bien increíble de los problemas más oscuros. (véase la Pascua)».

Siempre compartía con Fred mi último trabajo como director de musicales de primer y segundo grado y mi trabajo adicional como director coral para los musicales de la escuela secundaria. Él siempre respondía con mucho interés. Él también compartía sus últimos guiones y la complejidad del producto final. Este es solo uno de los varios ejemplos en los que escribió sobre su preparación para una nueva serie de espectáculos:

«Estoy intentando escribir algunos guiones nuevos. Como siempre, agradezco vuestras oraciones».

Hay que saber que Fred dedicaba innumerables horas a escribir sus guiones. Se podría pensar que para él era «fácil escribir», pero era una tarea compleja y se la tomaba muy en serio. Quería que cada palabra «contara». Sabía que sus palabras contribuían a formar la mente de los niños. Lo consideraba una enorme responsabilidad.

¿No es maravilloso que Fred me pidiera que orara por él mientras ministraba a los niños mientras escribía los guiones para su programa? Qué honor orar por un hombre que se dio cuenta de su importancia como colaborador en la ayuda a los niños. Fred se dio cuenta de que no podía escribir sin las oraciones de los demás. Era consciente de la responsabilidad que tenía... del poder de sus escritos.

En una carta, Fred compartió su entrevista con Katie Couric en The Today Show. «Katie Couric y yo hemos trabajado juntos antes, y ella se preocupa mucho por los niños... igual que tú. Somos una sociedad de cuidadores de tesoros, todos nosotros».

Como dije, realmente no hablábamos de política fuera del «ámbito educativo». En la época de nuestra amistad, quizá fuera ingenuo, pero creía que ambos partidos políticos tenían las mejores intenciones para los niños de nuestro país, por lo que la política no era un tema de conversación entre nosotros. Sigo creyendo que esto es cierto, pero parece que nos expresamos tanto sobre otros aspectos que ocultamos nuestra búsqueda conjunta de ayudar a los niños.

A veces es difícil «mantenerse al margen». Siempre me decepciona que el gobierno local o federal deniegue la financiación de una oportunidad educativa, pero lo que realmente me duele es la retórica que utilizan los líderes en la esfera pública, donde los niños están escuchando. Esto ha ocurrido en ambos lados del espectro político.

Como he mencionado en un capítulo anterior, he dedicado toda mi vida a los niños, por lo que cuando mi dedicación se ve empañada por palabras hirientes en la escena pública que los niños pueden escuchar, me siento profundamente preocupado. Ojalá los hogares pudieran proteger las mentes jóvenes de las palabras que se comparten en la televisión, pero mi recomendación de protegerlos de esta retórica a veces se ignora.

Creo que Fred respondería a cómo los políticos han utilizado palabras inapropiadas para «transmitir sus mensajes a nuestra nación de oyentes».

Las palabras importan.

Los insultos no son apropiados.

El odio hacia los demás no es apropiado.

Podemos hacerlo mejor.

En mi opinión, Fred «compartiría su preocupación» y la gente le escucharía. Nos hemos convertido en una sociedad en la que «todo vale». Espero que los líderes de nuestro país den ejemplo de un lenguaje que queremos que utilicen nuestros hijos. ¿Hay momentos en los que utilizamos por error un lenguaje inadecuado? Sí, pero el mundo actual ha permitido que sea algo común en lugar de excepcional. Como mínimo, podemos utilizar un lenguaje apropiado cuando los niños están escuchando.

Además, me pregunto por qué vivimos en una sociedad que siempre se centra en nuestra búsqueda de ganar, ganar y ganar. No se trata solo de una cuestión política, sino más bien de un problema social.

Escribí un libro infantil, *You Are a Masterpiece! (¡Eres una obra maestra!),* con ilustraciones de Shelly Bowden Dobi. El mensaje del libro es permitir que las recompensas intrínsecas sean el instrumento que hace que la vida sea exitosa. En otras palabras, disfruta del viaje que te ayudó a conseguir el «trofeo». Recuerda siempre que no puedes llevar el trofeo a todas partes, pero puedes llevar en tu corazón el recuerdo del duro trabajo que te costó ganar la recompensa extrínseca.

El trabajo duro se convierte en parte de lo que eres. El trofeo es algo que se acumula polvo en una estantería. Cuando nos centramos más en el camino, la decepción cuando fracasamos es más una experiencia de aprendizaje.

Los niños necesitan experimentar el fracaso y la decepción. Debemos proporcionarles las herramientas que les ayuden cuando fracasen. Al reconocer el fracaso y enseñarles a crecer a través de sus pérdidas, estamos preparando a nuestros hijos para la vida.

En este sentido, creo que debemos preguntarnos si nuestra «victoria» es una «victoria para todos».

Cuando ganamos, ¿ganan los niños hambrientos de los países del tercer mundo?

¿Ganan los niños cuyos padres no pueden pagar la guardería?

¿Ganan los niños cuyos padres no pueden pagarles el almuerzo?

¿Ganamos algo cuando se recortan los fondos para la programación infantil de PBS?

¿Realmente ganamos cuando otros sufren?

Creo que Fred haría estas preguntas.

Yo las planteo porque nuestros hijos no pueden hacerlo, y sin embargo, los niños parecen estar en el equipo perdedor en gran parte de nuestras victorias. Mis preocupaciones no están escritas en forma de ataque.

Tengan por seguro que mi intención es defender a los niños mediante preguntas reflexivas.

Fred se dirigió al Congreso para solicitar más fondos federales durante las primeras etapas de Mister Rogers' Neighborhood. Habló con calma, de forma directa y pacífica. Su presentación fue, desde el punto de vista financiero, un gran éxito. Fred y yo hablamos sobre su «negociación» con el Congreso cuando le compartí mis ideas sobre la preparación para una huelga del sindicato de maestros. Es importante señalar que los recortes financieros a las agencias que ayudan a los niños se han realizado en «ambos lados del espectro político» y han estado ocurriendo durante décadas.

A fin de cuentas, ¿es «ganar» la única forma de éxito que resuena en la cultura actual? Espero que no, y tengo esperanza. Creo que todos podemos unirnos en nombre de los niños para resolver muchos, si no todos, estos problemas.

Tengo esperanza.

En julio de 2025, una familia de la iglesia presbiteriana cantó una canción durante el servicio. La familia estaba formada por tres generaciones. Me dio esperanza ver a una familia de New Wilmington compartiendo su amor por Dios con la congregación. Los abuelos habían transmitido su amor por la música de la iglesia a sus hijos y estos, a su vez, habían transmitido ese mismo amor a sus pequeños. Fue un momento que conmovió a todos los asistentes. Representaba la ESPERANZA para el futuro.

Gracias a la familia Forsberg. Fred se habría llenado de esperanza por el mañana.

Sea como los Forsberg.

También he visto a una familia de tres generaciones trabajar junta en nuestro huerto comunitario, en los terrenos de nuestra iglesia. Fui testigo de cómo los abuelos daban ejemplo a sus hijos y nietos mientras cada generación plantaba, regaba, desbrozaba y cosechaba juntos. Gracias a las familias Romig y Hunter. Son un brillante ejemplo de ESPERANZA.

Sea como las familias Romig y Hunter.

Me maravilla el amor de otra familia por nuestra comunidad, que se manifiesta a través de los dones que Dios les ha dado. La familia Mohr también es de tres generaciones. Si pudieras ver al nieto de Jim y Jill Mohr, Johnny, abriéndose camino a través de diferentes oportunidades en nuestra iglesia, creo que lo verías a él, a sus abuelos y a sus padres como ejemplos brillantes de lo que es importante en nuestro mundo.

Sea como la familia Mohr.

Cuando menciono a estas tres familias que trabajan para hacer de nuestro «vecindario» un lugar mejor, creo sinceramente que Fred, si estuviera aquí físicamente, nos recordaría (como siempre hacía) que dediquemos más tiempo a la familia. Necesitamos un «espíritu familiar» que envuelva nuestro planeta. Fred consideraba a todos los habitantes de como su «familia televisiva». Él veía la «unidad familiar» como una solución sustancial a muchos de los problemas de nuestra sociedad.

Como mencioné anteriormente, hemos encontrado «vecinos» con quienes hablar sobre lo mucho que necesitamos a Fred en este momento. Creo que esa afirmación es muy reveladora. Cuando escucho ese sentimiento, siempre respondo diciendo que el mensaje de Fred puede transmitirse a través de nosotros. Podemos ser los portadores de su mensaje. Depende de nosotros. Todos los maravillosos contribuyentes a la sociedad que he mencionado en el capítulo anterior son ejemplos brillantes de lo que Fred aplaudiría. Solo tenemos que hacerlo más a menudo y de forma intencionada.

Además, creo que cuando cometemos errores, debemos pedir perdón. Ya sea en la escena política, en Hollywood, en la iglesia, en la escuela o en el barrio, siempre podemos pedir perdón. Sé que he cometido errores en los salones de clases y siempre he estado dispuesto a pedir perdón cuando ha sido necesario.

Es bueno admitir cuando se está equivocado. No es un signo de debilidad. Es un signo de crecimiento y de ser humano. Rezo para que cambie la marea y prevalezca la bondad. Podemos liderar con dignidad y carácter. Ser el «vecino» que Fred querría que fuéramos.

Como mencioné en un capítulo anterior, debemos imitar el silencio de Fred. Tómate tu tiempo para observar tu entorno. Escucha el ambiente. Escríbelo. Dibújalo. Compártelo. Si lo pensamos bien, gran parte del aprendizaje es gratuito.

Rezar es gratis.

Dibujar es gratis.

Escuchar y mirar son gratis.

Oler y saborear son gratis.

Pasear es gratis.

Ayudar a un vecino es gratis.

A veces es útil aburrirse. Cuando estamos aburridos, acabamos encontrando algo que hacer que es mucho más significativo que un teléfono móvil. Cuando estamos aburridos, la curiosidad puede tomar la iniciativa y llevarnos a un lugar que nos hace reflexionar.

Dos amigos míos, Gregg Behr y Ryan Rydzewski, han escrito un libro titulado *When You Wonder, You're Learning: Mister Rogers' Enduring Lessons for Raising Creative, Curious, and Caring Kids* (Cuando te preguntas, estás aprendiendo: las lecciones perdurables de Mister Rogers para criar niños creativos, curiosos y solidarios). (Hachette Book Group) Fueron ponentes invitados en el Westminster College y transmitieron el mensaje del título del libro con gran elegancia. Expresaron su mensaje como si Fred estuviera a su lado.

Les animo a leer su libro, con el prólogo escrito por Joanne Rogers, la esposa de Fred. Creo que expresa todo lo que un educador y un padre quieren que suceda en su salón de clases y en su hogar para ayudar a construir las herramientas que sus hijos necesitan para convertirse en aprendices y «vecinos» exitosos.

Sea conscientes. Fred era un ministro de la conciencia plena antes de que la conciencia plena se convirtiera en una «palabra de moda» para ayudar a todo el mundo a desarrollar habilidades de afrontamiento. Creo que Fred consideraba la «conciencia plena» como parte de la vida. Fred apreciaba los momentos de tranquilidad. Respirar. Hacer ejercicio (nadaba todas las mañanas). Rezar. Era un modelo de atención plena antes de que estuviera de moda. Tenemos que transmitir ese mensaje de alejarnos del «ajetreo de la vida» y tomarnos tiempo para estar presentes con el «regalo de la vida».

Fred, casi siempre, terminaba todas sus comunicaciones conmigo afirmando la importancia de mi vida. Aquí hay algunos finales de cartas que me parecen dignos de compartir:

«¡Qué afortunados son tus niños por tenerte (y obviamente tú sientes lo mismo por ellos)! Dar a los niños un comienzo feliz en su educación «formal» es un regalo que les has ofrecido para toda la vida. Bravo de nuevo, Todd».

«Esos estudiantes son muy afortunados de tenerte a ti y tu entusiasmo como parte de sus primeras etapas de vida. Te llevarán consigo todos los días. Hablando de influencia... esa es la mejor que puede haber».

«Los niños pequeños son afortunados de tenerte en sus vidas. Toda su actitud hacia el aprendizaje estará marcada para siempre por su relación contigo... Estás en mis oraciones. Gracias por tu encantadora carta.

Tu amigo,

Fred».

Estas palabras han dejado una huella imborrable en mi corazón. Sus palabras me dan el valor para ayudar a nuestras familias, hogares, ciudades, estados y países a convertirse en un lugar más civilizado para vivir y criar a los niños. En el prólogo mencioné que mi meta al escribir este libro era ayudarme a poner en perspectiva mi amistad con Fred para poder compartir su luz. Todo lo que tenía que hacer era abrir todas sus cartas y hacer un viaje al «pasado».

Todas las palabras que Fred escribió para mí también fueron escritas para ti. Estoy convencido de que, si Fred te hubiera conocido, habría compartido contigo algunos de los mismos pensamientos que te ayudarían en tu camino.

Considera sus palabras hacia mí como una conexión contigo. Deja que sus palabras te ayuden a ser un faro de luz para nuestros hijos.

Quizás este sea el momento de considerar salir de tu vida cotidiana de criar a tus propios hijos o nietos para marcar la diferencia con niños que están fuera de tu familia inmediata. Fred y yo solíamos hablar de cómo criar a los niños es responsabilidad de todos. No debemos dar la espalda a los problemas que tienen otros niños en la sociedad.

El hecho de que no sea tu hijo no significa que no sea tu problema.

Debemos ser parte de la solución.

Quizás te unas a una junta preescolar o escolar en tu comunidad para retribuir a las organizaciones que te ayudaron a criar a tus propios hijos.

Siempre puedes empezar a hacer donaciones económicas a organizaciones que apoyan a niños con cáncer u otras enfermedades.

Podrías convertirte en voluntario de bibliotecas públicas que promueven programas para niños.

Unirse al Rotary local puede ser algo que podría considerar, ya que es una organización que ayuda a niños cercanos y lejanos de muchas maneras.

Hay muchas vías que puede seguir para que su trayectoria esté más «centrada en los niños». Las posibilidades son infinitas.

Muchas de estas posibilidades requerirán «dejar el teléfono» y comunicarnos cara a cara. La tecnología es tanto una maldición como una bendición. Creo que muchas de nuestras respuestas al crecimiento social pueden abordarse de manera más eficaz a través de la interacción personal. Si reflexionas sobre todo lo que he compartido contigo acerca de Mike, Tracy, Jennifer, Stephanie, Mollie, Julie, Pete, Ellen y Fred, podrás reconocer el componente de «conexión humana» en todos sus éxitos. La tecnología tuvo muy poco que ver en todo lo que hicieron para difundir el mensaje de la bondad.

¿Qué querría Fred que hiciéramos? Intentemos avanzar en paz. Seamos instrumentos del «bien». Empieza con cada individuo. Hagámoslo. Hoy, no mañana. Ahora mismo. ¡Que este sea tu nuevo comienzo!

Paz,

Todd Cole, maestro de obras maestras

Epílogo

Es importante que todos los lectores de mis palabras sepan que soy consciente de que mi amistad con Fred era solo una de las muchas que él forjó y atesoró con personas de todo el país. Sí, compartíamos un amor único por servir a las vidas de los jóvenes, y creo que Fred quería celebrar esa coincidencia, pero él se acercó a muchas otras personas para forjar amistades profundas, genuinas y «auténticamente Fred».

Anteriormente, hablé de cómo Fred terminaba sus cartas con la palabra «Paz». Otras dos frases de despedida eran «Agradecido, Fred» y «Tu amigo, Fred». Cuán agradecido me siento por haber conocido a este hombre y cuán honrado me siento de que me llamara su amigo. Aunque quizá no lo conocieras personalmente, Fred también era tu amigo.

Sigue adelante y difunde la luz.

Este libro ha terminado, pero aún me queda mucho más por compartir. Aunque esta fue una parte muy importante del viaje de mi vida, hay más palabras que escribir cuando sea el momento adecuado. Por ahora, solo quiero que sepan que estoy agradecido por su e e disposición a leer sobre una amistad que me ayudó a crecer intelectual, espiritual, emocional y socialmente. Que su vida sea bendecida por todo lo que he compartido... la guinda del pastel.

P.D. A todos los que se tomaron el tiempo de leer mis palabras, les digo: «Adiós, mis queridos»

.

Libros que recomiendo sobre Fred Rogers

Muchas de las palabras compartidas por estos autores respaldan lo que Fred compartió conmigo. Los títulos de los libros 1 a 6 son libros infantiles y el resto de mi lista son para adultos. ¡Feliz lectura!

21. *Fred's Big Feelings: The Life and Legacy of Mister Rogers,* de Laura Renauld, ilustrado por Brigette Barrager. Atheneum Books for Young Readers

22. *Hello, Neighbor! The Kind and Caring World of Mister Rogers,* de Matthew Cordell. Neal Porter Books, Holiday House

23. *Mister Rogers' Gift of Music,* de Donna Cangelosi, ilustrado por Amanda Calatzis. Page Street Kids

24. *Mr. Rogers: Young Friend and Neighbor,* de George E. Stanley, ilustrado por Meryl Henderson. Aladdin Paperbacks

25. *The Story of Fred Rogers: A Biography Book for New Readers,* de Susan B. Katz, ilustrado por Can Tugrul. Rockridge Press

26. *Who Was Mister Rogers?* Por Diana Bailey. Penguin Workship: un sello editorial de Penguin Random House LLC, Nueva York

27. *The World According to Mister Rogers: Important Things to Remember,* de Fred Rogers. Hyperion Books

28. *The Simple Faith of Mister Rogers: Spiritual Insights from the World's Most Beloved Neighbor,* de Amy Hollingsworth. Integrity Publishers

29. *Mister Rogers' Neighborhood: Children, Television, and Fred Rogers,* de Mark Collins y Margaret Mary Kimmel, editores. University of Pittsburgh Press

30. *The Good Neighbor: The Life and Work of Fred Rogers,* por Max King. Abrams Press

31. *I'm Proud of You: My Friendship with Fred Rogers,* de Tim Madigan. Ubuntu Press, Los Ángeles

32. *Peaceful Neighbor: Discovering the Countercultural Mister Rogers,* de Michael G. Long. Westminster John Knox Press

33. *Revisiting Mister Rogers' Neighborhood: Essays on Lessons About Self and Community,* editado por Kathy Merlock Jackson y Steven M. Emmanuel. McFarland & Company, Inc., Publishers

34. *The Mister Rogers Effect: 7 Secrets to Bringing Out the Best in Yourself and others from America's Beloved Neighbor,* por la Dra. Anita Knight Kuhnley. Baker Books: una división de Baker Publishing Group

35. *Everything I Need to Know I Learned from Mister Rogers' Neighborhood: Wonderful Wisdom from Everyone's Favorite Neighbor,* escrito por Melissa Wagner, con ilustraciones de Max Dalton. Clarkson Potter/ Publishers

36. *Dear Mister Rogers, does it ever rain in your neighborhood? Letters to Mister Rogers,* de Fred Rogers. Penguin Books

37. *Fred Rogers: The Last Interview and Other Conversations,* con introducción de David Bianculli. Melville House

38. *The Last Interview and Other Conversations,* letras de Fred Rogers, ilustraciones de Luke Flowers. Quirk Books

39. *Mister Rogers' Neighborhood: A Visual History,* escrito por Melissa Wagner, Tim Lybargen y Jenna McGuiggan, con prólogo de Tom Hanks. Clarkson Potter/Publishers

40. *When You Wonder, You're Learning: Mister Rogers' Enduring Lessons for Raising Creative, Curious, Caring Kids,* de Gregg Behr y Ryan Rydzewski. Hachette Book Group

Agradecimientos

Gracias a Gregg Behr y Ryan Rydzewski por permitirme utilizar su libro en mi texto.

Gracias al Instituto Fred Rogers por concederme el privilegio de utilizar citas que él escribió en sus cartas dirigidas a mí.

Gracias a *Fred's Big Feelings: The Life and Legacy of Mister Rogers,* de Laura Renauld, con ilustraciones de Barrager, Atheneum Books, por el privilegio de compartir una paráfrasis de sus palabras sobre la forma que tenía Fred de aliviar la ira.

Gracias a la familia de Robert Berks por permitirme utilizar una foto mía posando junto a la estatua de Fred en Pittsburgh.

Gracias a David Newell por permitirme compartir una de las cartas que me escribió.

SOBRE EL AUTOR

Todd Cole es maestro de niños de todas las edades. Cole fue maestro de primer grado durante 25 años y de cuarto grado durante 9 años. Considera que la escuela primaria Laurel es un lugar sagrado, un lugar donde los maestros se reúnen para ayudarse mutuamente a enseñar a los niños, no el currículo. Tras jubilarse, se embarcó en una nueva aventura: enseñar a los estudiantes a convertirse en maestros en su alma máter, el Westminster College. Ha sido profesor de la Facultad de Educación durante 8 años. Considera que esto es una continuación de su labor de «enseñar a los niños».

A Todd le gusta difundir su amor por la literatura infantil participando como invitado mensual en el programa WFMJ TODAY en Youngstown, Ohio. Este es su vigésimo quinto año en el Canal 21. Escribe editoriales trimestrales sobre todo lo relacionado con la educación para periódicos locales. A menudo se puede encontrar a Todd como lector invitado en bibliotecas, guarderías y eventos especiales en toda la zona oeste de Pensilvania.

Su trabajo como rotario del Club Rotario de New Wilmington es algo que le importa mucho. Se trata de una organización sin ánimo de lucro que ayuda a personas de aquí, de allá y de todas partes. Le anima a que se informe sobre esta organización en su propia comunidad.

Cole ha escrito dos libros infantiles, *You Are a Masterpiece! (¡Eres una obra maestra!),* con ilustraciones de Shelly Dobi, y *Peace Is.../Paz Es,* escrito junto con su perro, Titan. Todd también ha escrito dos libros de «consejos para maestros»: *50 Shades of Teaching* y *50 More Shades of Teaching/50 Sombras (más) de Enseñanza.* Dos de estes libros fueron traducidos por Debra Sanchez, quien también tradujo la parte en español de este libro.

Cole es un miembro activo de su iglesia como presbítero, miembro del equipo de adoración, del coro y de la junta de preescolar. Su participación en la iglesia le ayuda a «seguir respirando». Es una fuente que le ayuda a expresar el amor de Dios por todas las personas.

Todd es un antiguo alumno activo del Westminster College, donde ha sido presidente del Consejo de Antiguos Alumnos e invitado en la emisora Titan Radio. El Westminster College es el espacio físico que le ayudó a forjar amistades para toda la vida que pueden considerarse su «familia elegida».

Todd comparte su hogar con su golden retriever, Titan (que lleva el nombre de la mascota del Westminster College). Titan estaba a los pies de Todd mientras escribía este libro. Es su compañero inseparable y puede hacer sonreír a los habitantes de New Wilmington cuando recorren la ciudad en un descapotable para disfrutar de la agradable brisa en un día soleado.

ABOUT THE TRANSLATOR

Debra R. Sanchez has moved over thirty times. She earned her B.A. in communications and writing from Westminster College. She and her husband have three adult children and seven grandchildren…so far.

She teaches writing workshops, provides writing coaching, and hosts writing retreats. She also is a freelance editor and a translator of a wide variety of topics, including numerous books.

She is the exclusive translator for Tree Shadow Press. Their Spanish language books can be found in the "Libros en Español" page of Tree Shadow Press. https://www.treeshadowpress.com

Her writing has won awards in various genres, including children's stories, poetry, fantasy, fiction, and

creative nonfiction. Several of her plays and monologues have been produced and published. Her other works have been published in literary magazines, newspapers, and anthologies.

For more information, visit her webpage
www.debrarsanchez.com
and follow her on Facebook: @DebraRSanchez

SOBRE LA TRADUCTORA

Debra R. Sanchez se ha mudado más de treinta veces. Es licenciada en Comunicación y Escritura por el Westminster College. Ella y su marido tienen tres hijos adultos y siete nietos... hasta ahora.

Ella ofrece talleres de escritura, asesora a escritores y organiza retiros de escritura. También es editora independiente y traductora de una amplia variedad de temas, incluidos numerosos libros. Ella es la traductora exclusiva de Tree Shadow Press. Los libros en español de Tree Shadow Press pueden encontrarse en la página "Libros en Español" de Tree Shadow Press.

https://www.treeshadowpress.com

Sus obras han sido premiadas en varios géneros: cuentos infantiles, poesía, fantasía, ficción y no ficción creativa. Varias de sus obras de teatro y monólogos han sido producidas y publicadas. Sus otras obras se han publicado en revistas literarias, periódicos y antologías.

Para más información, visite su página web:
www.debrarsanchez.com
y sígala en Facebook: @DebraRSanchez

www.ingramcontent.com/pod-product-compliance
Lightning Source LLC
LaVergne TN
LVHW010059110826
845155LV00028B/402

* 9 7 8 1 9 4 8 8 9 4 4 7 0 *